The Rock Synthesizer Manual

A Revised Guide for the Electronic Musician

by Geary Yelton

ROCK TECH PUBLICATIONS
Woodstock, Georgia

© 1986 by Geary Yelton

Published by Rock Tech Publications
171 West Putnam Ferry Road
Woodstock, Georgia 30188

Printed and bound in the United States of America.

Library of Congress Cataloging in Publication Data

Yelton, Geary
    The rock synthesizer manual.

    Bibliography: p. 123
    Includes index.
    1. Synthesizer (Musical instrument) I. Title.
ML1092.Y44   1986   789.9'9   86-4918
ISBN 0-914283-25-1 (pbk.)

CONTENTS

FOREWORD

Though the synthesizer in one form or another has been with us for decades, its true public acceptance has only been a matter of years. This recent exposure of electronic music is in no small measure due to the unique combination of influences exerted by the world of rock music. Having widespread popular appeal, coupled with a lack of inhibitions imposed by formal musical structures, the world of rock recording and performance has been fertile ground for the extensive use, and creative growth of electronic music. Working outside of the academic community's closed environment, rock synthesists have followed a creative evolutionary course that is directed in large part by the relatively quick feedback provided by the listening public. The popularity and sales of a variety of electronic music experiments reflect the public's like (or dislike), and therefore the success or failure of many audio and music adventures. No other field of music gives the public as large a voice in the creation of the art it consumes.

And what are the elements of this creativity? As always, composition is the most important one, but following closely is the "sound" of the recording. For years, the sound of a record was limited to the catalog of conventional effects available in the recording studio. Live performance was even more constrained. In recent years, though, the techniques of synthesizers have exploded out of the limited domain of the keyboardist to encompass all aspects of instrumentation and vocals. From guitar synthesizers to electronic drums, the ensemble has been sonically restructured. Vocalists have access to a variety of digital sampling devices and sound modification equipment, with capabilities extending from simply improving a performance to the ability to create new frontiers of vocal sound.

Even the realm of the recording engineer and producer has been altered dramatically. The application of VCA and ADSR technology into every module of the most popular professional recording desks signifies the evolution of primarily rock-derived synthesizer techniques into other aspects of recording. Composition and the role of drummers have also been radically altered, owing to the adoption and evolution of sequencing techniques already in use by synthesists for over a decade. The development of the tapeless MIDI recording studio shows how strongly electronic synthesizer techniques and style have redefined the compositional and recording process.

Live performance has also undergone a similar evolution, with advanced sequencing and complex digital and analog sounds, once limited to the recording environment, becoming commonplace.

No musician considering serious work in rock music today can afford to be lacking in knowledge of the tools and techniques of this most important aspect of contemporary music. As we enter the age of all-digital synthesis and recording, such a background will be far more important than many of the more conventional tape recording technologies that we take for granted today. Since synthesis and sound sculpting are becoming more than extentions of the recording process, a thorough understanding of synthesizers will become even more essential.

— LARRY FAST

INTRODUCTION

Hello, and welcome to the second edition of *The Rock Synthesizer Manual*. There are many good reasons to read this book. Perhaps you're new to the world of electronic music, and you want to unlock the mysteries facing you for the first time. Maybe you've been playing a synthesizer for years, but you never really took the time to learn your way around its control panel. Or could be you're just curious about recent musical technology, and you'd like to increase your understanding of electronic instruments. Whatever your excuses, you've come to the right place.

Synthesizers are made in a great variety of shapes, sizes, and configurations. They can produce and reproduce an enormous range of sounds, both musical and non-musical. Like the piano 250 years ago, the synthesizer is both a technological wonder and, as time will tell, potentially the greatest advance in musical tools of this century. And as anyone can tell you, they make great toys. But more than that, they're serious, sophisticated musical instruments to be studied and cherished. In the right hands, and with sufficient understanding, a synthesizer is a potent stimulant for creativity.

A lot has happened in the world of music synthesis since the previous edition of *The Rock Synthesizer Manual.* The sound of synthesizers and other electronic instruments has become commonplace in popular music. The Musical Instrument Digital Interface has become a very real standard. Digital FM synthesizers and sampling instruments have become everyday tools to the keyboard-playing musician. An increasing number of musicians are gaining a working knowledge of computers, as much out of musical necessity as the need to explore new territories. If you don't keep up, you get left behind.

If you're like most electronic musicians, you collect isolated scraps of information and, all too often, blatant misinformation about synthesizers and related technology, from other musicians, from magazine articles, from manufacturers' clinics, and possibly from introductory courses at school. All too many "synthesists" just blindly stumble around until they discover a few interesting tone colors, or they rely on sounds created by people who specialize in synthesizer programming. Where do you turn when you have questions? Most books on electronic music are either too sketchy or too scholarly to be very useful. Though the situation is improving, the majority of synthesizer books are written as manuals to accompany specific models. This one was written as an introductory course, a practical reference, and an operator's manual for virtually any synthesizer, regardless of make or model.

The Rock Synthesizer Manual's goal, simply stated, is to give you a detailed introduction to the art and technology of electronic music. It's mostly about analog synthesis, but a lot of the information you'll find here can be applied to various forms of digital synthesis. No matter what type of music you play, the basics are all the same. Like any musical instrument, you really need to learn what your synthesizer can do to realize your full potential as a synthesist.

The Synthesizer Revolution

The technology of music is in constant flux. Hybrid instruments, digital samplers, FM synthesizers, computer music on the radio — how do you keep up? New keyboard instruments appear every month. Things are changing so fast in the world of electronic music, even the experienced synthesist is faced with a bewildering array of equipment and new synthesizing techniques to assimilate at an unprecedented rate. Rapid progress is the norm, but things haven't always been that way.

Electronic musical instruments have been with us since 1899, when William Duddell, an English physicist, used a keyboard to control musical tones produced by a carbon arc lamp. The next year, Thadeus Cahill completed his prototype of the Telharmonium, a gigantic electronic music system featuring additive synthesis and a touch-sensitive keyboard. The final version weighed at least 200 tons and had to be moved by an entire train. Thanks, in part, to the invention of the vacuum tube oscillator in 1915, electronic instrument designers sprang up throughout the '20s and '30s. The theremin, first seen in the United States in 1927, had a definite impact on 20th century music. (You may have heard a theremin in the Beach Boys' "Good Vibrations".) It was controlled by the motion of the performer's hand in the space surrounding it. The Ondes Martenot, a French electronic instrument introduced in 1928, is still taught in some French music schools. That same year saw the invention of the Trautonium, with a sawtooth oscillator, filters, and a contact ribbon for control.

The first real synthesizers appeared in 1945. One was the Hanert Electronic Orchestra, a roomful of equipment which read graphite marks on paper cards. Another, Hugh Le Caine's Electronic Sackbut, featured a velocity-sensitive keyboard, portamento, and continuous timbre control. Ten years later, the RCA Synthesizer, designed by Harry Olson and Herbert Belar and reportedly costing a quarter of a million dollars, became the first analog instrument under digital (numerical) control. It was a monophonic giant with tube oscillators, amplifiers, and filters, controlled by rolls of punched paper tape. The RCA Synthesizer wasn't played in real time, but recorded its sounds directly onto phonograph records. The musicians' union led a successful crusade against its commercial development, and RCA donated the RCA Mark II to the Columbia-Princeton Electronic Music Center.

ANALOG SYNTHESIZERS

In 1963, Don Buchla began using voltages to control hand-crafted electronic music modules. He built the first instrument to incorporate voltage-controlled oscillators, amplifiers, filters, and a sequencer. Buchla's instruments had little effect on popular music because they were designed specifically for experimental composition and because they didn't have traditional keyboards. The next year, Bob Moog brought electronic music synthesis out of the laboratory and into the mainstream. Moog's voltage-controlled synth modules were integrated into a system controlled by a keyboard, and by 1967, musicians

everywhere started hearing about Moog synthesizers. People like Walter (now Wendy) Carlos and the Beatles used them in the recording studio, and the world began to take notice.

Rock musicians, always on the lookout for new and exciting sounds, embraced the synthesizer immediately. Electric instruments were the everyday stuff of rock, and the sound of the synthesizer just sort of fit in naturally. In the late 1960s, synthesizers were complicated, bulky instruments that required wiring together lots of different modules to produce good sounds. Those early modular instruments were quite temperamental and not well suited to live performance. Oscillators drifted with the slightest change in temperature, and patchcords were prone to breakage.

A few adventurous performers, notably Keith Emerson of Emerson, Lake, and Palmer, went to great trouble and expense to drag an impressive array of customized electronic gear onto the concert stage, only to achieve a very limited range of sounds. But they were completely new sounds — sounds never before heard by rock audiences in a performance setting. "Synthesizer" became a buzzword of the times.

It wasn't long before other rock musicians began to perform on synthesizers. Back in those days, a synthesist's worth was at least partially measured by the sheer cubic volume of his equipment. A hundred patchcords strung among banks of knobs, switches, and flashing lights had an undeniable impact on the impressionable consumer. When the monster was tamed, it was electrifying, but several synthesizers were needed to obtain any variety of tone colors. Drastically altering patches was just too complicated to be done in real time.

Most musical instrument makers had little faith that synthesizers would gain any real popularity. Still, traditional instrumentalists again tried to suppress their use, for fear of being replaced by machines. (They didn't understand, and the slower ones still don't, that real musicians play them.) By 1970, performance-oriented, portable synthesizers from ARP and Moog in the U.S., and EMS in England, became available in music stores. The Minimoog and ARP 2600 were quick to catch on. The synthesizer revolution had begun.

Eventually, expensive modular instruments more or less fell by the wayside as these more affordable, more manageable, internally hard-wired versions began to flood the market. When just a few years earlier hardly anyone knew what a synthesizer was, it became necessary artillery in every rock keyboardist's arsenal. The majority of keyboard players just memorized the settings for a handful of the most useful sounds and never progressed beyond that point. The more inventive synthesists continued to forge ahead, exploring new timbral territories.

Up until the mid-Seventies, the synth was strictly monophonic, playing only one voice at a time. Monophonic instruments have been around for centuries, but for musicians with backgrounds in piano and organ, the situation was confining. Their synthesizers were, after all, keyboard instruments. Something inevitably had to be done. In

response to their needs, after years of research and development, the polyphonic synthesizer was born. Some expected that the polysynth would enable them to recreate complex multitrack compositions in real time. That capability was still years away. Nonetheless, the development of polyphonic synthesizers made it possible to weave textures and harmonic accompaniment that even a dozen monosynths could never realize in live performance.

HYBRID SYNTHESIZERS

The mid-Seventies also marked the beginning of the microchip revolution. Musical electronics became considerably more compact, and prices began to plummet. More sophisticated hardware became available to struggling musicians everywhere. Scaled-down synthesizers could be had for the cost of an electric guitar, and a digital computer that might have once been the size of a car and cost a great deal more, was reduced to a single circuit board costing a few dollars.

Synthesizer manufacturers were quick to incorporate digital technology into their products. E-mu was the first company to build a microprocessor into its instruments, soon to be followed by Oberheim. Oberheim also introduced the first truly polyphonic (and multi-timbral) synthesizers with partial patch memory as an option. But it was Sequential Circuits who made synthesists sit up and take notice in 1978 with their Prophet-5, the first user-programmable polyphonic synthesizer with complete patch programs accessible at the touch of a button. It even tuned itself, all thanks to its built-in microprocessor. A few noteworthy instruments of that time missed the digital bandwagon. The Polymoog (weighing in at 82 pounds) was the first polysynth with a split, velocity-sensitive keyboard, and Yamaha's CS-80 (a mere 220 pounds) had a keyboard with pressure-sensitivity, both instruments without benefit of computer control.

Almost every voltage-controlled synthesizer with the ability to memorize patch programs is an analog/digital hybrid. The sound-producing electronics may be analog, but the on-board microprocessor and software run the show. Many instruments can store and recall over 100 patches. They're usually shipped from the factory with a full complement of pre-programmed sounds. To the majority of keyboardists, this often means never having to learn to program synthesizers. To others, patch memory is an excellent way to permanently preserve a wide timbral palette of their own design, or duplicate and recall the best sounds of their favorite performers. With a modern synth, you can create an individual instrumental vocabulary. No two synthesizers ever have to sound exactly alike.

SEQUENCERS

Sequencers have also made their mark on electronic music. Sequencers are most often used to play back a series of notes automatically, like a player piano. Analog sequencers store a sequence of independently programmable control voltages,

which are used to control a monophonic synthesizer's oscillator pitch (and possibly other parameters). A typical analog sequencer has from one to three parallel rows of knobs or sliders, with typically from eight to 24 pots in each row. Each pot (potentiometer) can be manually set to the desired control voltage level. Now that digital sequencers are cheaper to build than their analog predecessors, however, analog sequencers are practically extinct.

A polyphonic digital sequencer can memorize riffs, phrases, even whole songs to be played back on one or more synthesizers. You can buy sequencers packaged as independent controllers, but many popular instruments have sequencing functions built right in. Some sequencers let you enter notes and rests stepwise, one at a time, but most of them record and play back anything you play on the keyboard, exactly as it's played. The best modern multitrack sequencers record every aspect of performance, including what notes you play, how hard you hit the keys, modulation and pitch bend, patch changes, and individual parameter changes. You can record at any tempo, edit your mistakes, overdub, transpose parts, swap instrumental voices, and play your performance back at any speed. There was a time when music played with sequencers sounded robotic and mechanical, but those days are past. Music recorded and played back by a digital sequencer today can be indistinguishable from a live performance.

DRUM MACHINES

Drum machines, variously called beat boxes, rhythm units, or percussion sequencers, have also gained a position of importance in electronic rock and other musical forms. A drum machine contains an integral multitrack sequencer for memorizing and arranging rhythmic patterns, and is often programmed in stepwise fashion. A few can be programmed from a synthesizer keyboard in real time, even memorizing how hard the keys are struck. Some drum machines duplicate the sounds of acoustical percussion instruments by analog or digital synthesis, and others contain the digitally-recorded sounds of real drums. Most can be synchronized with sequencers for simultaneous playback.

MIDI

Of all the technological innovations to have an impact on electronic instrument design in the last few years, the greatest has been the Musical Instrument Digital Interface, otherwise known as MIDI. MIDI is a hardware standard and a digital communications protocol which lets synthesizers share information with other synthesizers, with sequencers, with drum machines, and with personal computers. Since its introduction in 1983, MIDI has been adopted by every major manufacturer of electronic musical instruments.

Before MIDI, there was very little standardization of control signals from one brand to the next. If you wanted a sequencer for a particular synth, you probably had to get it from the same manufacturer. Now you can buy a complete synth minus the keyboard from one company, a keyboard from another, a sequencer from another, and a drum machine from still another, and tie them together to form a digital recording and performance system, all for less money than the cheapest polyphonic synthesizer cost in 1980. Best of all, you can use almost any popular computer as a central controller or even as a source of synthesized sounds.

Consumer demand has forced electronic instrument makers to implement MIDI on all their new products. Musicians have always insisted on new and better ways of making music, and forward-thinking instrument designers must fulfill those needs. Now you can pick and choose from a variety of personal computer interfaces and programs for controlling synthesizers. A single MIDI interface provides 16 polyphonic channels for playing multiple instruments simultaneously.

Perhaps the most exciting software lets you use your computer as a multitrack sequencer. Sequencer programs are generally more flexible than dedicated sequencers, and they can be easily and less expensively updated at any time. Patch librarian programs let you save hundreds or thousands of stored sounds (patch programs) on a single computer disk for instant recall, far surpassing the internal storage of any synthesizer. Another type of MIDI software analyzes what's played on the synthesizer keyboard (or any other MIDI controller) and converts it to standard music notation, which can often be further edited and then printed on paper. Voice editor programs display parameter information on the monitor screen, helping the synthesist visualize the patch programming process.

Some voice editors even draw waveforms and envelopes on the screen. Many synths only allow access to one parameter at a time via the front panel controls, but a voice editor lets you see and edit multiple parameters at the same time. Some computers support software which combines all these functions, serving as a sequencer, patch librarian, score transcriber, and voice editor. MIDI lets you do things with a computer and synthesizers that would have cost at least a dozen times as much just five years ago.

DIGITAL SYNTHESIZERS

Computers have been used to generate musical sounds for around 30 years. Over the decades, researchers have developed dozens of methods for digitally synthesizing waveforms. General purpose computers have no oscillators or envelope generators, but these functions can be digitally simulated by software and converted to sound. A sound can be specified as a series of numbers, each one representing a fraction of the entire waveform. Ground-breaking contributions to the field of computer-generated music have been made by Max Mathews of Bell Laboratories and John Chowning of Stanford University.

One innovation with a tremendous impact was the introduction of user-programmable digital FM synthesizers. These instruments, beginning with the Yamaha DX7 and DX9, produce complex timbres by modulating sine waves with other sine waves generated by a microprocessor. There's a popular notion that FM synthesizers are difficult or impossible to program unless you have a degree in physics. Most players seem reluctant to learn to program their Yamahas because so few really understand FM synthesis (and Yamaha's one-parameter-at-a-time data entry doesn't help). They fear what they don't understand, so they shy away from learning even the basics. Sure, FM is something new, but it wasn't that long ago when analog synthesis seemed just as universally mysterious. If you have a firm grasp of the fundamentals of musical sound, there's no reason why programming FM synthesizers should be beyond your reach.

Another digital synthesis scheme is the method used by Casio CZ synthesizers, called phase distortion synthesis. Complex waveforms are created by recalling simple waveforms and reproducing them at a varying rate. The resulting waveforms are combined for greater complexity.

One of the oldest methods of digital synthesis is a technique known as additive synthesis or Fourier synthesis. An additive synthesizer combines the simplest elements of sound, building complex waveforms from scratch by specifying the dynamic levels of individual harmonics. Analog (subtractive) synthesis, on the other hand, begins with complex waveforms and filters out unnecessary overtones. Additive synthesis lets you reproduce more natural-sounding instrumental timbres, but the techniques involved are very tedious and time-consuming. Each harmonic must be specified in terms of frequency, phase, and amplitude, and how those properties change over time. Without the aid of the computer, impersonating acoustical instruments with additive synthesis takes practically forever.

SAMPLING INSTRUMENTS

Sampling instruments are capable of recording acoustical sounds and playing them back by keyboard control. With a digital sampler, you can actually play the sound of real violins, human voices, even entire orchestras. Typically, a few seconds of an instrumental sound are recorded at one frequency, then digitally "sped up" for higher pitches and "slowed down" for lower ones. Some digital samplers let you record multiple samples across the keyboard at different dynamic levels for more realistic reproduction.

The use of sampling keyboards in rock music goes back at least as far as the Mellotron, a well known rock mainstay of the late Sixties and early Seventies. The Mellotron was a polyphonic, analog keyboard instrument containing many short lengths of recording tape, one for each key, which were pulled over recording heads when its keys were depressed. Each set of tapes contained recordings of an acoustical instrument or an ensemble playing or singing all the needed pitches. Each tape always began at the beginning, reproducing the attack portion of each note, and returned to the beginning when its key was released. Another instrument, the Chamberlain, worked by the same principles, using loops of tape instead of fixed lengths. These instruments were subject to mechanical difficulties and their tapes would simply wear out.

In 1979, the Fairlight CMI, from Australia, was the first synthesizer with the capacity to record sounds digitally. Sound sampling soon became available on New England Digital's Synclavier II, but like the Fairlight, its expense was beyond the budgets of all but a few musicians. 1981 heralded the appearance of E-mu's Emulator, a digital sampling instrument geared to the performing keyboardist. A couple of years later, the Kurzweil 250 made its first appearance, impressing people not only with the striking realism of its grand piano and other instrumental sounds, but with its piano-like keyboard action as well. Even as the technology grows more sophisticated, prices continue to fall. By the time the Emulator II was introduced in 1985, working musicians and amateurs could buy an Ensoniq Mirage for under $1700. Now traditional synthesizer makers like Sequential and Roland are building powerful samplers for under $2500.

THE FUTURE

The future of electronic music is never very far away. The perpetual introduction of new hardware and software shows no sign of subsiding, which means increased capabilities and lower prices for everyone. It seems strange that in an age where electronic musical instruments are compatible enough to communicate, the actual techniques of synthesis have gotten so diverse that it's nearly impossible for one person to gain a working familiarity with them all. Even as MIDI instruments become friendlier toward one another, the number of digital schemes used to generate sound is expanding at an accelerating rate. Instruments using FM, Fourier, and phase distortion methods of digital sound generation have barely scratched the surface.

Digital technology in general will have an even greater impact on future synthesis. Already, advanced samplers can manipulate stored waveforms in a number of ways, including analog signal processing and structural re-synthesis. Recorded sounds can be taken apart and reassembled to create sounds never heard on Earth. As sampling gets cheaper, it will be easier for the amateur or student musician to buy an instrument which sounds and plays like a fine piano, but looks like a synthesizer, than to buy a real piano. Both at home and in the studio, digital recording of acoustical sounds will become commonplace as technology advances and prices continue to fall.

Personal computers will play an increased role as their operating systems become more intuitive and more musicians discover their advantages. Some of the most exciting musical research and development being done today is in software design for personal computers. With the power of modern microprocessors, the flexibility and user friendliness of sequencers and other tools are only limited by the imaginations of their programmers. It won't be long before software incorporating artificial intelligence techniques and amazing advances in hardware simplify the whole process of music production, so musicians will be less concerned with data entry, channel assignment, memory limitations, and how to pay for it all.

Throughout the history of mankind, the craft of instrument making has been dependent on the latest technology available to the instrument maker. When the first drum was constructed, its builder probably used the most advanced materials available to him. Pianos were impossible until the appropriate technology was developed. The 20th century has given birth to electronic musical instruments, and those instruments, in one form or another, are no doubt here to stay. Who knows what unpredictable discoveries await us? Perhaps someday, someone will invent the perfect synthesizer, one that does everything all the others can do for a fraction of the cost, and everyone will buy that one. Then again, maybe not. Musicians always have, and always will, looked for new ways of making music. Stay tuned — the future awaits.

Electronic Sound

THE BASICS OF SOUND

Synthesizers manipulate the building blocks of sound. To understand just how synthesizers work, you have to know at least a little about what makes one sound different from another. Let's go over the basics: When piano strings or vocal cords vibrate, our ears perceive these vibrations as sound. Each individual vibration is called a wave or a cycle. The rate of vibration is the frequency of that sound, measured in cycles per second, called Hertz (abbreviated Hz). One cycle per second is 1 Hz, and a thousand cycles per second is one kiloHertz (1 kHz).

Okay, how about some examples? If you strike a tuning fork whose pitch is A-440, it vibrates 440 times every second. It completes one cycle every 1/440th of a second. If you play an A above middle C on a well-tuned piano, the strings vibrate back and forth 440 times a second. When you play the same pitch on a saxophone, the reed also vibrates at a rate of 440 cycles per second. If you place any of these sound sources in front of a microphone, it produces a tiny electrical current that alternates every 1/440th of a second. When

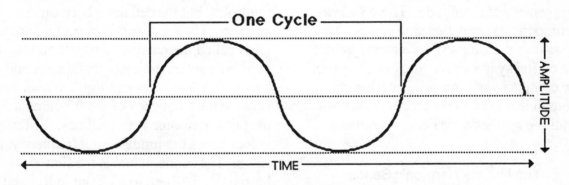

Sine Wave

A sound's frequency determines its pitch. Pitch is expressed as musical notes: A, A#, B, C, and so on. Pitch indicates a note's relative position on the scale. Higher frequencies produce higher pitches, and lower frequencies produce lower pitches. Musical instruments, especially synthesizers, produce a wide range of pitch.

that current is amplified and applied to a loudspeaker, the speaker also vibrates back and forth 440 times a second. Measure that sound with a digital frequency counter, and you get a reading of 440 Hz. The pitch, of course, remains an A. Get the picture?

Just as every musical sound has frequency, it also has amplitude. Amplitude is a measure of strength, loudness, or intensity. The amplitude of an acoustical source depends on how hard it vibrates. Each cycle has a constantly changing amplitude. More importantly, every musical sound has tone color or timbre (pronounced tam' br). The timbre of a trumpet, for instance, is one of the characteristics that makes it sound different from an electric guitar. Timbre is determined by the shape of each wave, called the waveform. A waveform is a graphic representation of a single wave. When you draw a waveform, you plot its variations in amplitude over the time it takes to complete one cycle.

Every single note played on any instrument actually produces a complex combination of simple waves, each different in frequency and amplitude. These individual components are called sine waves. The sine wave is the simplest waveform. With some digital synthesizers, you can construct more complex waveforms by combining various sine waves. This process is known as additive synthesis, or Fourier synthesis.

The Natural Harmonic Series

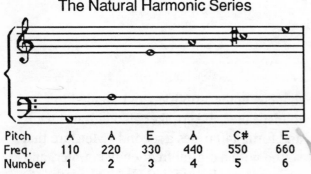

Pitch	A	A	E	A	C#	E
Freq.	110	220	330	440	550	660
Number	1	2	3	4	5	6

HARMONICS

When we say that a musical tone has a particular frequency, we're really talking about the fundamental frequency, or fundamental, of that tone. Of all the sine waves in a complex waveform, the fundamental usually has the lowest frequency and the greatest amplitude. Other frequencies in a complex sound are called partials or overtones. If these overtones are exact multiples of the fundamental frequency, they're called harmonics. A sound's harmonic content is sometimes referred to as its spectrum.

One reason that analog synthesizers sound so pure is because the harmonics they produce are exact multiples of the fundamental. Most musical sounds produce overtones which aren't quite mathematically precise multiples, but we call them harmonics anyway. The relationship between harmonics is called the natural harmonic series. The harmonic series indicates that the second harmonic (also known as the first overtone) is twice the frequency of the fundamental, the third harmonic is three times, the fourth is four times the fundamental frequency, and so on. The fundamental is the first harmonic. It's hard to pick out individual overtones by ear, because they're usually not as loud as the fundamental. They're very important, though, because their number, frequencies, and relative strengths determine the timbre of a musical sound. The greater the number and strength of the overtones, the more complex a waveform becomes.

SOUND SOURCES

Oscillators are the main sources of synthesizer sounds. Most synthesizer oscillators generate complex waveforms. Instead of producing acoustical waveforms the way a vibrating object does, they generate electrical waveforms. Just as sound has frequency and amplitude, so does alternating current. You can't hear an oscillator's signal until it's amplified, and the amplified signal vibrates a loudspeaker. If the frequency is between approximately 20 Hz and 20 kHz, it's an audio frequency. When an oscillator's frequency is below the range of human hearing (sub-audio), it has no apparent pitch, but it's still useful to the synthesist.

limited variety of waveforms. Two complex waveforms, pulse and sawtooth, are almost always available. Some oscillators also offer a simpler waveform called a triangle.

The sawtooth wave, also called the ramp wave, is the only basic synthesizer waveform which contains every harmonic of the natural harmonic series. Its high harmonic content gives the sawtooth a bright, full sound. As the harmonic number (first harmonic: 1, second harmonic: 2, etc.) increases, the corresponding overtone has less and less amplitude. The amplitude of

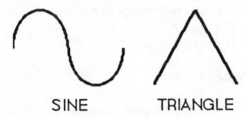

SINE   TRIANGLE   PULSE   SAWTOOTH

SYNTHESIZER WAVEFORMS

A sound's harmonic structure depends on its waveform, so the waveform determines the tone color. Some waveforms are rich in harmonics, while others have relatively few. The fundamental frequency is always the strongest component in basic synthesizer waveforms. The upper harmonics grow gradually weaker as they ascend up the harmonic series. Certain harmonics may be absent altogether. Analog synthesizer oscillators offer a

each harmonic can be expressed as a fraction of the amplitude of the fundamental. In a sawtooth wave, the amplitude of the second harmonic is 1/2 that of the fundamental frequency. The third harmonic is 1/3, and the fourth is 1/4 the amplitude of the fundamental. When you monitor a sawtooth wave on an oscilloscope, it's shaped like a sawtooth no matter what its frequency. If you listen to positive and negative sawtooths, there's no audible difference.

Positive Sawtooth Wave

Negative Sawtooth Wave

The pulse wave, also known as the rectangular wave, is the most useful for synthesizing a variety of tone colors, because you can change its shape. A pulse wave oscillator is constantly turning itself on and off at a particular frequency. Its instantaneous amplitude is either up or down, positive or negative, but virtually never transient. By changing the shape of the pulse waveform, you alter its harmonic structure. That's accomplished by varying the pulse width.

The pulse width, or duty cycle, is the proportion of one cycle that's "on". Pulse width is usually expressed as a percentage of the complete cycle, or sometimes as a fraction. The fraction's denominator tells us which harmonics are missing from the pulse wave's spectrum. Each different pulse width has a slightly different tone color. By changing the duty cycle, we alter the harmonic content. (Like positive and negative sawtooth waves, inverted pulse waves are harmonically identical. A 60% pulse sounds like a 40% pulse, and a 25% pulse sounds like a 75% pulse.) Most synthesizer oscillators offer a broad range of pulse width, as much as from 0 to 100%. Of course, if your synth has continuously variable pulse width instead of fixed duty cycles, you have a greater assortment of timbres at your disposal.

Pulse Waves

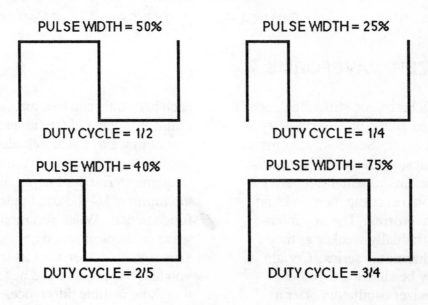

PULSE WIDTH = 50%

DUTY CYCLE = 1/2

PULSE WIDTH = 25%

DUTY CYCLE = 1/4

PULSE WIDTH = 40%

DUTY CYCLE = 2/5

PULSE WIDTH = 75%

DUTY CYCLE = 3/4

When the width of a pulse wave is half a complete cycle, the waveform is called a square wave. A square wave is simply a pulse wave with a 50% duty cycle. It's so useful that it's considered a basic waveform. The square wave has only odd-numbered harmonics. Because its upper overtones are stronger, its sound is even brighter than a sawtooth.

The triangle wave, sometimes called the delta wave, is also made of odd harmonics only. Its overtones are much weaker than the overtones of a square wave. As a result, the fundamental is very strong and the timbre is less harmonically dense. By mixing a triangle wave in with a more complex waveform, you can emphasize one particular harmonic without mucking things up with unwanted overtones.

PHASE

When two VCO signals are mixed together, they may be out of phase. They begin their cycles at slightly different times. Even with the greatest care in tuning, you might still hear them drifting in and out of phase with one another. Phase is defined as the position of a wave in time, or the instantaneous relationship between waves in time. The phase angle is the degree of one cycle's completion at any given point. The difference in the phase angle of the two waves is called phase shift.

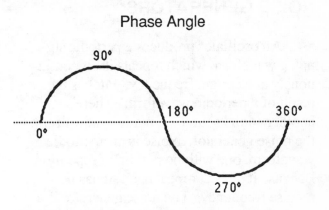

Phase Angle

Whenever two oscillator signals are even slightly out of tune with each other, their phase shift is constantly changing. They alternately cancel and reinforce one another. When one wave reaches its maximum positive value at the same instant another wave reaches its maximum negative value, the result is zero amplitude. Their opposite polarity makes them cancel each other out. Conversely, when two waves match up, in phase with one another, their amplitude is increased. When the phase relationship of two waves is between these extremes, various harmonics are emphasized and de-emphasized in sequence.

Most synthesizers have a phase sync switch for synchronizing two oscillators. When it's on, one oscillator's signal remains perfectly in phase with the other oscillator's signal, eliminating phase shift. If the oscillator that's forced into sync is tuned an interval above the other, it will phase-lock itself to the closest harmonic from the lower oscillator. Instruments with digitally-controlled oscillators don't have sync switches, because their oscillators are always perfectly synchronized. To simulate the effect of oscillator phase shift, a chorusing circuit is often built into synths with DCOs.

NOISE GENERATORS

An oscillator produces a periodic signal, a waveform which repeats itself continuously at a certain frequency. Pitch is the result of a periodic waveform. There's another sound source on many synthesizers: the noise generator. Noise is an aperiodic waveform, one with no pattern of repetition. Because it doesn't repeat itself, it has no precise frequency. The noise generator is a synthesizer's primary source of unpitched sound.

The noise generator on some synthesizers produces white noise, also called white sound. Just as white light contains all colors of the visual spectrum in seemingly balanced proportion, white noise contains a random distribution of all audible frequencies. Every frequency has equal amplitude. The odds of finding any certain frequency are equal to the odds of finding any other frequency. We hear white noise as a constant "ssshh" sound, like an FM radio between stations.

Because of the way our ears respond, the higher frequencies in white noise seem louder than the lower ones. Pink noise is created by filtering out some of the upper bands. Pink noise has equal amplitude in every octave. It sounds deeper than white noise, more like the sound of a waterfall. Most synthesizers feature a pink noise generator.

AMPLIFIERS AND ENVELOPES

Every sound has a contour. When you play a musical tone, it usually takes a moment to reach its peak intensity. This moment is called the attack of that sound. The attack often tells us more about how a note is played than any other parameter. When a tone ends, it may take a second to die away completely, or it may stop suddenly. This final decrease in loudness is called the decay. The attack and decay characterisitics, along with other variations in loudness in between, make up a sound's envelope, or dynamic contour.

Like audio waveforms, envelopes can be graphically represented as amplitude plotted against time. Unlike audio waves, which usually occur many times a second, envelopes happen one at a time and last for the duration of each note or sound event. Envelope and timbre are the two most obvious differences between the sounds of one musical instrument and another. All sounds undergo dynamic changes in amplitude, no matter how quick or drawn out they are. Synthesizers, of course, produce envelopes electronically.

Envelope generators, sometimes called transient, function, or contour generators, let you shape synthesizer sounds simply by turning knobs, pressing switches, or adjusting sliders. The envelope generator produces a changing control signal which is most often used to control the synthesizer's amplifier and filter.

VOLTAGE-CONTROLLED AMPLIFIERS

Almost every synthesizer contains at least one voltage-controlled amplifier (VCA). A VCA's output characteristics are controlled by a signal from another circuit. VCAs are a bit different from audio amplifiers. Most amplifiers, like the one in your stereo system, increase the intensity of input signals. The volume control determines how much a signal is amplified before it's routed to the speakers. A voltage-controlled amplifier, on the other hand, never increases a signal's amplitude (with very few exceptions). At best, a signal entering the amplifier has the same amplitude when it comes out.

Instead of amplifying a signal's amplitude, a VCA attenuates it. Think of it like a water faucet. When you turn a faucet wide open, all the water flowing into it rushes out at full force. Turning it down attenuates the flow of water, restricting the amount that can pass through the faucet. A VCA works the same way. Closing it decreases the level of signals passing through it. When it's completely closed, signals can't get through. When it's open, signals pass unattenuated.

The amplifier controls the gain of its input signal. Gain is the ratio between the amplitudes of the input and the output signals. A amplifier's gain can be continuously varied by the strength of a control signal. When no control signal is present, audio signals can't pass through the amplifier. As the value of the control signal increases, the gain increases, the amplitude of the output signal increases, and the sound grows louder. The strength of the audio signal changes instantly and accurately whenever the amplifier's control signal changes.

TRIGGERS, GATES, NOTE ONS & OFFS

Whenever you strike a key on an analog synthesizer keyboard, it puts out a pulse that, in effect, tells the envelope generator, "This is the beginning of an envelope." That pulse is called a trigger, because it triggers the envelope generator to begin its attack. Some instruments use positive voltage triggers, while others use negative switch triggers. As long as the key is held down, the keyboard also produces a fixed signal called

a gate. The gate tells the envelope generator, "Don't stop." When the key is released, the gate ceases, and the envelope generator goes into its final stage. In many instruments, the gate doubles as the trigger, indicating both the beginning and the end of a note event. Modern MIDI synthesizer keyboards produce similar signals using digital commands. When a key is depressed, a Note On signal is generated. When the key is released, a Note Off signal is sent.

ENVELOPE GENERATION

The envelope generator is the amplifier's number one control source. Its changing level tells the amplifier when to open, how far to open, and when to close. An amplifier circuit can't spontaneously change a signal's strength all by itself. It needs a control input. The amplifier produces dynamic changes in gain in response to signals from the envelope generator.

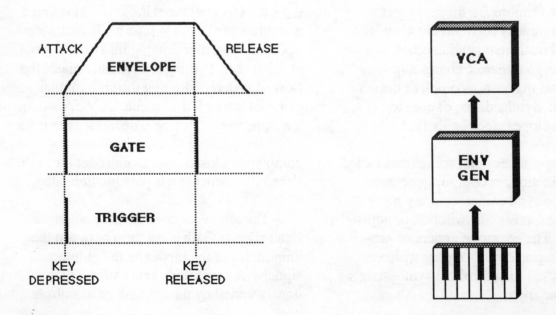

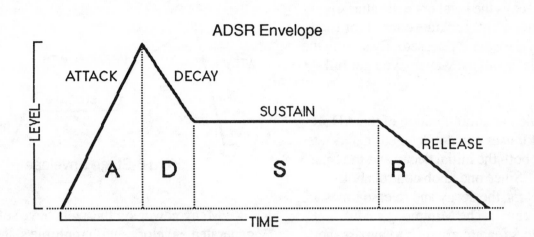

ADSR Envelope

Several envelope generator types are found on different synthesizers. The most common variety is the ADSR generator. It produces an envelope in four stages: attack, decay, sustain, and release. When used to control an amplifier, the attack setting determines the time it takes an audio signal's level to go from zero to maximum when a key is struck. As soon as the level peaks, the initial decay stage takes over. It controls how long it takes to fall to the sustain level. The position of the sustain pot determines how much signal can pass through the amplifier while the note is held. (Don't confuse sustain with what a piano pedal does — that actually controls final decay, or release.) When the gate ends or a Note Off signal is received, the release stage takes over, often regardless of whether the other stages are complete. The amplifier's output then drops back to zero at a rate determined by the release setting.

Notice that the attack, decay, and release stages all govern lengths of time, but the envelope generator's sustain setting determines a control signal level. When the sustain is turned all the way up, the initial decay has no effect. If the sustain level is zero, the amplifier closes at a rate governed by the decay setting. Unless the key is released before the decay begins, the release stage is effectively bypassed.

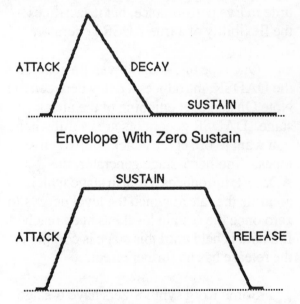

Envelope With Zero Sustain

ADSR With Full Sustain

The simplest type of envelope generator has just two stages, attack and release. It's called an AR generator, and it operates like an ADSR generator with full sustain. After the attack stage, the level remains at its peak until the Note Off, and the release stage begins. A three-stage generator called an

ADR decays the level once the attack is complete, with a separate control for final decay if the note is released. By setting the initial decay all the way up, you get full sustain.

Another simplification of the ADSR generator uses one pot, labeled "decay", to control both the initial decay and the final release. Since one knob controls both parameters, the decay and release times are always equal. The Minimoog's ADS generators feature a switch to bypass the release stage altogether. When it's switched on, the decay pot controls only the initial decay, and the release time is zero. For a synth without programmable patch memory, this type of arrangement may save time in live performance, but it sacrifices the flexibility of a true ADSR generator.

One type of 5-stage envelope generator, the DADSR, introduces a delay between the Note On and the beginning of the attack stage. DADSR generators are useful when you want to offset the attacks of two envelopes. Another 5-stage generator, the ADSDR, introduces a fourth stage which controls the rate at which the level decays to zero once the sustain level has been reached. If a note is held until this stage is complete, the release has no further effect.

Some Korg synthesizers have 6-stage envelope generators. After the attack, the envelope decays to a level called the break point, then moves to the sustain level at a rate determined by a setting labeled "slope". The sustain may be higher or lower than the break point, but if it's the same, the break point and slope are effectively bypassed. The envelope generator's output remains at the sustain level until the release takes effect.

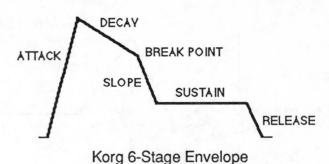

Korg 6-Stage Envelope

Many newer synthesizers have software-generated envelopes with multiple stages defined by the user. Yamaha DX synthesizers have 8-stage envelopes which let you define every level and the periods of time taken to get from one level to another. A common ADSR generator has three user-definable rates (attack, decay, and release) and one user-definable level (sustain). With an ADSR, you have no control over the level reached during the attack, usually the maximum, or the level reached during the release, usually minimum. The envelope generators on DX synths let you control four rates and four levels. The attack doesn't necessarily build up to the maximum level, and the release doesn't always have to drop the level down to zero. If the final level is higher than zero, however, the operator may drone on unimpaired until the beginning of the next envelope.

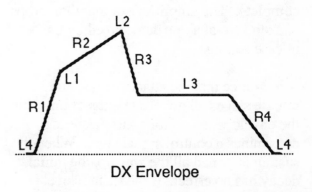

DX Envelope

Here's how a DX envelope works: When a key is depressed, the envelope generator signal goes to Level 1 at a rate determined by the Rate 1 setting. Then it immediately changes to Level 2 at Rate 2. If Level 2 is higher than Level 1, the output increases. If it's lower, it decreases. If Level 2 is the same as Level 1, this stage is bypassed. After Level 2, the output goes on to Level 3 at Rate 3 and stays there until a Note Off signal is received. When the key is released, the output changes to Level 4 at Rate 4. Level 3 is like the sustain level of an ADSR generator, and rate 4 is identical to the release stage.

The digitally-generated envelopes of Casio CZ synthesizers have eight rates and eight levels. This design lets you produce rather complex envelopes. When a Note On is received, the envelope signal goes to Level 1 at Rate 1, just like the DX envelope. You can specify which level is the sustain level. You can also determine which level is the envelope's end point, so an envelope doesn't have to use all 16 stages.

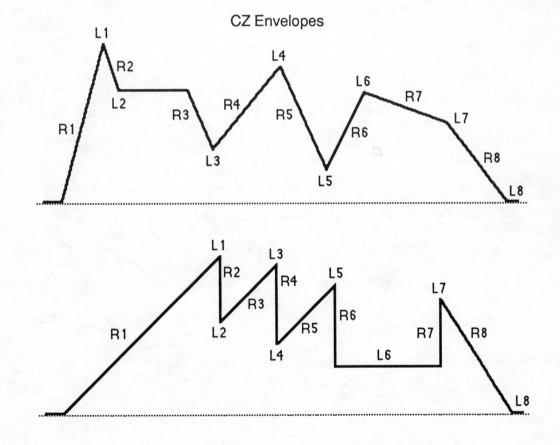

CZ Envelopes

Suppose you feed an audio signal into the filter. If you turn up the resonance, the frequencies closest to the cutoff frequency are regenerated; that is, they're fed back to filter. All other frequencies are attenuated, and the cutoff slope becomes steeper. At high resonance settings, the cutoff frequency becomes greatly exaggerated, and any change in cutoff frequency is also exaggerated.

Most synthesizers have a self-oscillating filter. When the resonance is turned up full, it generates a sine wave at the cutoff frequency, even without an audio signal input. If you apply a keyboard control signal to a self-oscillating filter, it can be played like an audio oscillator. Like most oscillators, it usually has a standard sensitivity of one volt per octave.

FILTER ENVELOPES

An envelope generator is a synthesizer filter's primary source of control signals. Just as a sound's amplitude changes over its duration, so does its timbre. Some harmonics appear only at the beginning of a sound. These brief harmonics are called attack transients. You can recognize an instrumental sound by its timbral envelope, also called harmonic contour.

The majority of synthesizers have two envelope generators: one to control the amplifier and another to control the filter. When an ADSR generator controls a lowpass filter's frequency, the attack determines how long it takes the filter to open to its maximum brightness. The peak

brightness depends on the setting of the envelope amount control, also called envelope depth, intensity, level, or modulation. This pot controls the extent of the envelope generator's influence on the filter. The minimum filter cutoff depends on the position of the initial filter frequency control, but the maximum cutoff is usually determined by a combination of the initial frequency, the envelope depth, and sometimes the amount of keyboard control signal being routed to the filter.

When the attack stage is complete, the cutoff frequency falls to the sustain level at a rate governed by the decay setting. The sustain stage holds the brightness at a steady level until the key is released. Then the release stage controls how quickly the filter returns to its initial cutoff frequency. If the filter is already wide open, the envelope generator has no audible effect.

SUMMARY

An envelope generator is a control source. Its changing signal can change the filter's cutoff frequency. The filter governs what harmonics can pass, and the oscillator waveform determines what harmonics are present before filtering. Filtering has no effect on a simple sine wave, except to strengthen or weaken its fundamental frequency, because it has no overtones to filter out or emphasize. The main purpose of a filter, controlled by an envelope generator, is to reshape the spectra of complex waveforms.

MODULATION

Controlling modulation is an important part of playing the synthesizer. To modulate, quite simply, means to change or modify some audible characteristic. When you modulate a synthesizer's audio signal, you're changing something about the way it sounds. A changing control signal can modulate oscillator frequency, pulse width, filter frequency, or amplifier gain. An important modulation source is the low-frequency oscillator, or LFO, sometimes called the sweep or modulation generator.

A low-frequency oscillator generates periodic waveforms in the sub-audio range. A manual frequency pot often controls the rate of oscillation. Its range may be typically from 20 Hz down to .1 Hz (one cycle every 10 seconds), but the range varies from one synth to another. All LFOs produce sine or triangle waves, which are essentially the same for modulation purposes. Many LFOs also generate square waves, and some offer positive and/or negative sawtooth waves. A modulation depth control, usually a continuous controller separate from the LFO section of the control panel, governs how much a given characteristic is modulated by the LFO.

2 Hz LFO Sine Wave

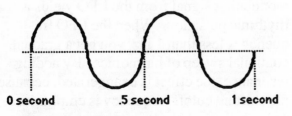

0 second   .5 second   1 second

VIBRATO

When an LFO control signal modulates the frequency of an audio oscillator, its pitch follows the shape of the modulating waveform. If the LFO's output is a sine wave or a triangle wave, the pitch rises and falls at a regular rate. At the proper rate and depth, this type of modulation is called vibrato.

Many performers rely on vibrato to add expression to their performance. A violinist employs vibrato with a shaking motion of the hand as it applies pressure to the string. A singer gently fluctuates the pitch of his or her voice. A synthesist uses an LFO to modulate oscillator frequency. The LFO frequency controls the rate of modulation, and the strength of its signal controls its depth.

Because vibrato alters frequency, it's one type of frequency modulation, abbreviated FM. Frequency modulation is any deliberate change in the frequency of an audio signal. Extremely complex timbres can be produced by modulating one audio waveform with another (more on FM later). Classical trills can be realized by modulating an audio oscillator with a low-frequency square wave. A low-frequency sawtooth can modulate an audio oscillator to create classic science fiction sound effects.

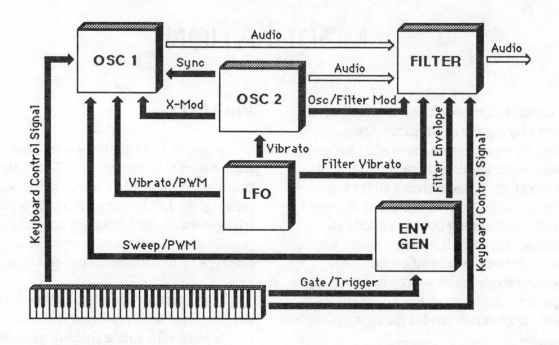

PULSE WIDTH MODULATION

Many synths employ pulse width modulation, or PWM, to modulate oscillator waveforms. Pulse width can usually be changed either manually or by a control signal. A pulse wave's duty cycle can be varied by an envelope over the duration of each note, or it can be swept gradually by an LFO. As the waveform is modulated, the amplitudes, frequencies, and phase of the harmonics change dynamically. If the pulse width is modulated by a low-frequency sine or triangle wave at a certain depth and frequency, a quasi-chorusing effect is possible.

Pulse width can sometimes be modulated by an envelope generator. When you strike a key, the envelope settings determine how the waveform changes. You've got to be careful when using large amounts of pulse width modulation, or when the initial width is rather narrow. If the pulse width is

pushed below zero or beyond 100%, the whole waveform is cancelled out. A narrow pulse wave should be modulated to a wider pulse width, and vice versa. Unless, of course, you want the cancelling effect.

FILTER MODULATION

Filter modulation can be useful. Shaping a sound's harmonic contour with an envelope generator is just one type of filter modulation. When an LFO sine wave modulates filter frequency, at the proper depth and rate, the result is filter vibrato. Filter vibrato is indispensable for synthesizing certain sounds, such as flute. A slower modulating signal from the LFO yields a rhythmic pulsation. When the LFO frequency is less than 1 Hz, you get a gradual, continual sweep of harmonics. By adding resonance, the effect is exaggerated, because the shifting cutoff frequency is emphasized.

Most filters have a control input from the keyboard. This allows the filter to track, or follow, the keyboard control signal, much as an oscillator does. As the notes played on the keyboard ascend and descend, their brightness can be made to increase and decrease. The depth of tracking is usually adjustable. With full one-volt-per-octave tracking, you can play a filter like an oscillator.

AMPLITUDE MODULATION

A number of synthesizers provide for certain types of amplitude modulation, or AM. The simplest AM occurs when you vary the gain of an amplifier with a low-frequency (5 - 10 Hz) waveform. Any audio signal passing through the amplifier fluctuates in intensity, resulting in an effect called tremolo. The tremolo rate is controlled by LFO frequency, and the depth, by the amplitude of the modulating signal.

Any time you modulate one audio frequency with another, you produce sidebands. Sidebands are frequencies not found in either signal, but resulting from their combination, called sum and difference tones. These frequencies are literally the mathematical sums and differences of the modulated frequency and the modulating frequency. For example, if a 440 Hz sine wave is modulated by a 110 Hz sine wave, additional frequencies of 550 Hz (440 Hz + 110 Hz) and 330 Hz (440 Hz - 110 Hz) are generated. Sum and difference tones are produced for each harmonic of both waveforms. If either signal is harmonically complex, many sidebands are produced. The resulting sound is rich in non-harmonic overtones, frequencies which aren't multiples of the fundamental frequency. If simpler waveforms are used, fewer sidebands are generated. The number of sidebands depend on the spectra of both the modulating signal, called the program or modulator, and the signal being modulated, called the carrier.

Amplitude modulation is accomplished on some synths by a circuit called a ring modulator or a balanced modulator. Ring modulation is most often used to synthesize clangorous sounds, metallic timbres constructed entirely of non-harmonic overtones, such as gongs, bells, and chimes. A ring modulator is a specialized kind of amplifier. When a modulating signal is applied, the circuit exhibits alternately positive and negative gain in equal proportions — balanced modulation. Both the program and the carrier are suppressed, leaving only the sidebands at the modulator's output.

SAMPLE & HOLD

Several synthesizers feature sample & hold, a control source useful for producing random-sounding changes. Your synth may let you control oscillator frequency with sample & hold, but usually, its signal modulates filter frequency. Sample & hold appears as an LFO waveform on a number of instruments.

In this case, "sample" has nothing to do with digital recording. Every time a clock signal advances the sample & hold, it "takes a snapshot" of a signal input, sampling its instantaneous amplitude at that precise moment, holding it there until the next tick of the clock. If the signal is coming from a noise generator, the resulting output could be any value within its bandwidth. Each time the clock ticks, the output changes, generating a series of random control signals. If the input is a low-frequency positive sawtooth and the sampling rate is faster than the input frequency, the output may be a repetitive series of ascending steps. In a limited way, sampling LFO signals can simulate sequencing. Unfortunately, most sample & holds only sample noise, not oscillator signals.

FM SYNTHESIS

Using frequency modulation as a means of tone production is familiar territory to anyone seriously involved in computer music. Basically, when you take a simple audio waveform and modulate its frequency with another simple audio waveform, the result is a more complex waveform. A greater number of sidebands are produced than with amplitude modulation, and unlike AM, the sidebands vary in intensity. The harmonic spectrum of the resulting sound can be altered by changing the relative frequencies and amplitudes of the modulating waveform (the modulator) and the waveform being modulated (the carrier). If the modulator is an exact multiple of the carrier, basic synthesizer waveforms can be created.

Until computer circuits became economical, building commercial FM synthesizers just wasn't practical. Analog FM synthesis is much too unstable. Analog oscillators have a tendency to drift, and if an oscillator's frequency drifts even slightly, the precise mathematical relationship between the carrier and modulator changes drastically. Digital circuitry is capable of much greater precision. Modern digital FM synthesis techniques were pioneered by Dr. John Chowning in 1973. His methods have been further refined by others, but most notably by Yamaha, resulting in their phenomenally successful DX series of digital FM synthesizers.

OPERATORS

Instead of analog oscillators, VCAs, and ADSR generators, each voice of the Yamaha DX7, for example, has 6 operators. An operator is a software-generated sine wave oscillator paired with its own amplitude envelope. Operators are combined to create complex waveforms — that's the basis of FM synthesis. Operators are either carriers or modulators. Carriers are the operators which produce the sound, and modulators control the sound's timbre.

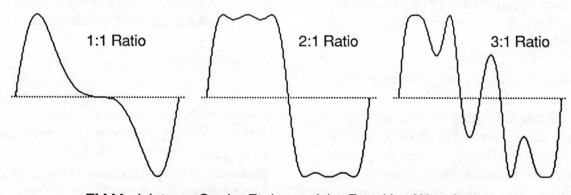

1:1 Ratio   2:1 Ratio   3:1 Ratio

FM Modulator to Carrier Ratios and the Resulting Waveforms

A tone's pitch depends on the carrier frequency, with the modulating operators determining waveform and frequency content. You can hear only carriers, but you hear the effect of modulators. Frequency modulation occurs when you patch a modulator's output to a carrier's input. DX synthesizers let you set the initial output level of each operator, as well as control its dynamic output with the envelope generator. Operators may be turned on and off as required. By varying the output of the modulator with an envelope, the resulting timbre is dynamically controlled.

The timbre of most acoustic instruments changes over the duration of each note. A good additive synthesizer lets you control the pitch and amplitude envelope of each harmonic, so that individual harmonics may vary in both pitch and loudness over time. FM synthesizers duplicate such dynamic changes in timbre by varying modulator output. The strength of each modulator signal is controlled by an envelope generator, and for more expressive dynamic control, by keyboard velocity and pressure. Operator output may also depend on what part of the keyboard is played, if keyboard level or rate scaling are part of the patch. To most ears, the resulting signal may actually seem more acoustic in nature than analog electronic sounds, thanks to the dynamic nature of its waveform.

The frequency ratio between a carrier and its modulator determines its initial waveform. Changing the relative frequencies of the carrier and modulator, like changing their relative amplitudes, also results in dynamic control of the spectrum. By using an envelope generator to control the frequency of each operator, the harmonic content of each sound event can change over its duration.

KEYBOARD SCALING

The way operators interact may also depend on pitch, or more specifically, the position of the note being played on the keyboard. There's a parameter called keyboard rate scaling, which affects envelope values. When an operator's rate scaling is higher than zero, its attack and decay times are shortened as you ascend up the keyboard. This feature is not unlike key follow on other synthesizers. There are eight levels of rate scaling. At a setting of 1, attack and decay times at the top of the keyboard are increased by a value of 6. At the highest setting, rates are increased by a maximum value of 42.

Keyboard level scaling is a little more complicated. When the note is above or below a user-defined break point, level scaling boosts or cuts operator output level. If the operator is a carrier, the position on the keyboard determines the carrier's loudness. If the operator is a modulator, the total harmonic content may depend on which key is played. Keyboard level scaling controls whether each operator grows stronger or weaker as you ascend up the keyboard from a particular note.

Any key can be the break point. To set the level scaling, you define a curve on each side of the break point that determines how much an operator's output is increased or decreased as the pitch rises or falls. The curve can be extreme, or linear, for split keyboard simulations and other exaggerated effects. Or it can be a natural, exponential curve. Exponential curves are good for subtle timbre changes over the range of a synthesized instrument. Both kinds of curves can be positive if you want operator level to grow stronger as the pitch ascends, and negative if you want it to get weaker. Warning: Thoughtful keyboard rate and level scaling of all six (or even all four) operators can result in powerful FM sounds.

ALGORITHMS

Operators are arranged in various combinations called algorithms. In computer science, an algorithm is a set of procedures for carrying out a certain operation. An FM algorithm (as the term is used by Yamaha) is nothing more than a configuration of operators (see diagram). The greater the number of algorithms at your disposal, the greater the variety of sounds you can achieve. The DX7 offers 32 algorithms, mapped out on the front panel in order of potential harmonic complexity. Letting modulators modulate one another (stacking) or letting a modulator modulate itself (feedback) allows even more sound-producing flexibility by harmonically enriching the modulating waveforms. Many DX algorithms differ by how they're stacked, but some differ only by which operator includes feedback. When all operators are carriers, you can achieve additive synthesis.

Each algorithm represents a method of combining elements that make up a complete sound. Most acoustic instrumental sounds

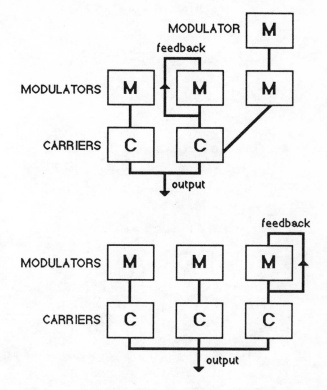

are a composite of numerous elements. The sound of a snare drum, for example, is a combination of the crack of the stick hitting the drum head, the overall vibration of the head, the resonance of the shell, and the rattle of the snare. A violin sound includes the friction of the bow, the vibration of the string, and the resonances inherent in different parts of the violin's body. Using FM synthesis, you may synthesize each portion of a composite sound by modulating a single carrier. Each operator contributes to the final result. One modulated carrier might duplicate the primary vibration of a drum head or a violin string, for instance, and other carriers account for resonant frequencies within the instrument. That's what's so great about FM synthesizers: You can concentrate on the fine details that breathe life into musical sounds.

Control

CIRCUIT CONTROL

Electronic music came into existence when musicians began to experiment with vacuum-tube circuitry. Actually composing music from those primitive circuits was mostly a tedious and time-consuming process that eventually involved splicing together hundreds of pieces of recording tape. Electronic musical instruments were designed and built, but with the exception of the electronic organ, very few gained any real popularity. Life is much simpler today, thanks in large part to the concept of using voltage to control electronic music circuits.

With voltage control, various circuits within a synthesizer can communicate and interact with one another. When you depress a key on an analog synth keyboard, it puts out a corresponding voltage. Exactly how many volts depends on which key is depressed. That control voltage (abbreviated CV) tells the oscillator what frequency to generate, and therefore, what pitch you hear. The voltage produced by one circuit (in this case, the keyboard electronics) determines the operating characteristics (frequency) of another circuit (the oscillator).

In an analog synth, voltages control changes in pitch, loudness, and timbre, giving you command of expressive capabilities. You might achieve the same ends by manually turning knobs or pushing sliders, but human hands just aren't fast or accurate enough to compete with voltage control. Even if they were, you'd have to grow a few extra limbs to handle everything. Voltage control can be thought of as a super-human extension of manual control. Digital control is even faster and more precise than voltage control.

For the past few years, just about every synthesizer made contains at least one microprocessor. This small computer often takes on the responsibilities of circuit control, producing digital signals which may be converted to control voltages by digital-to-analog converters. In some synthesizers, the computer generates digital equivalents of analog circuits, bypassing voltage control entirely. Voltage control and digital control each have advantages and limitations which must be considered when designing (or buying) a synthesizer.

Every sound, musical or otherwise, has parameters which make it unique. A sound's parameters are its variable characteristics, or the values (the numbers, if you will) used to synthesize that sound. Loudness, frequency, spectrum, and duration are all parameters that make up a musical sound. Synthesizer controls are used to manipulate the parameters of electronically-produced sound.

Synthesizers generate two kinds of analog or digital information: audio signals and control signals. What makes audio and control signals different is how they're used. Whether a signal is one or the other often depends on where it's going, rather than where it's coming from. An oscillator doesn't care if it's generating an audio signal or a control signal. If it's generating an audible waveform, it's an audio source. If it's controlling another circuit, it's functioning as a control source.

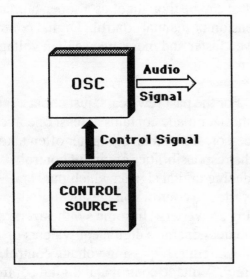

Because an analog synthesizer oscillator can be controlled by a voltage, it's called a voltage-controlled oscillator, or VCO for short. Most VCOs have a sensitivity of one volt per octave. This means that the pitch changes one octave for every one volt

change in the control voltage. Every equal increase (or decrease) in control voltage causes a doubling (or halving) of frequency. If you decrease the voltage by two volts, for example, the pitch drops two octaves. Any change in the control voltage changes the oscillator frequency.

A digitally-controlled oscillator, or DCO, is directly controlled by numbers generated by the synthesizer's on-board computer, in response to information from the keyboard. The oscillators produce analog signals, but they are controlled by digital signals. These days, most synths have VCOs which respond to signals that start out digital but are changed to voltages before they reach the oscillators.

In theory, just about any function which can be controlled manually can be controlled by a voltage. In most analog synthesizers, voltages control only four parameters:

1) oscillator frequency
2) oscillator pulse width
3) filter frequency
4) amplifier gain

PATCHING

Playing a synthesizer is more than just playing a keyboard. It involves connecting circuits, a process called patching, by routing both audio and control signals. Programming sounds is accomplished by patching circuits and functions together. In the old days, you had to use patchcords to connect various modules to get the desired sound. Most often, patching is now as simple as tweaking a few knobs and pressing a few switches. In most synthesizers, commonly used signal paths are provided by internal wiring among the circuits. The keyboard sends signals to the oscillators to control their frequency. The oscillator signal is routed to the filter, then to the amplifier. The synthesizer's microprocessor is responsible for processing signals and routing them to their respective destinations.

Control signals can be added together at their destination's control input. That way, one signal routed to an oscillator, for example, controls pitch, and another controls vibrato. Their sum total at any given instant determines the circuit's operating characteristics. If the voltage from any one source is increased, the total control input is likewise increased. Audio signals are combined by an internal audio mixer.

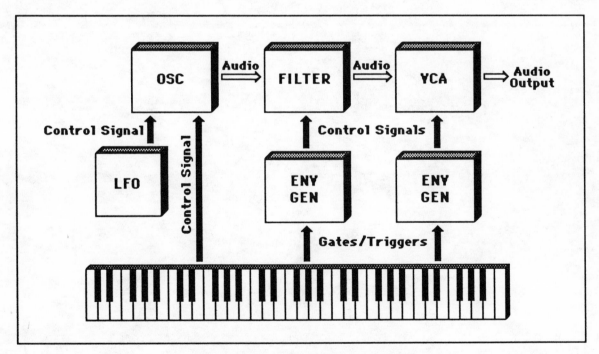

Synthesizer Signal Routing

KEYBOARDS AND VOICES

The keyboard lets the performer control the pitch and duration of synthesized sounds, and often other parameters. It may look exactly like an organ or piano keyboard, and it plays more or less the same. When you depress a piano key, you cause a small hammer to strike the appropriate strings. When a key is pressed down on an electronic organ, it switches on a corresponding fixed-frequency tone generator. When you strike a synthesizer key, the keyboard generates an electrical signal.

A synthesizer keyboard puts out a signal that depends on which key is struck. If it's an analog keyboard, it may also generate a trigger, which appears momentarily at the instant the key is depressed, and a gate, which lasts as long as the key is held down. When the key is released, the gate stops, but the control voltage is held constant by a circuit which remembers the last key depressed. Modern synth keyboards digitally generate Note On and Note Off commands. Digital circuitry scans the keys at a very high rate to determine which ones are depressed at any given moment.

A synth keyboard is often referred to as a keyboard controller. It's one of several controllers which can supply synth circuits with the electrical impulses they need to make music. The keyboard serves as the primary link, connecting the performer with the oscillators and the envelope generators. Because this particular control device takes such a familiar form, a synthesizer can be quite articulate in the hands of almost any experienced keyboard player.

If you're accustomed to playing an acoustic piano, one of the first differences you'll notice about a synth keyboard is its action. There's no physical mechanism to be moved as in the piano, so springs or weights are attached to each key to offer some resistance. Without them, the action would be too light, and the keys would move too easily to play accurately. The action varies from one synth keyboard to another, too. Some are stiff, some are squishy, some are just right. If your new synthesizer's keyboard feels strange and alien to you, don't worry. With practice, you'll get used to it.

Not all keyboards are created equal. One obvious difference is their length. Some are three octaves or less, while most have five or more octaves. But the essential difference among synth keyboards, or synthesizers for that matter, is whether multiple voices can be played simultaneously. Older synths have keyboards which produce a single control voltage/trigger/gate combination to control one sound at a time. These instruments are monophonic synthesizers, or monosynths, meaning that they have only one voice. In recent years, they're considered somewhat obsolete, but there are plenty of good used monosynths available at prices almost anyone can afford.

Polyphonic synthesizers, or polysynths, have two or more voices. The majority have from six to sixteen. In most synthesizers, the voices are homogeneous, meaning they all respond to the same patch information, so they all sound more or less alike. If you have a polysynth producing a piano patch, every key sounds like a piano. Some instruments feature a unison mode, which allows you to play every voice simultaneously with each key depression. A 6-voice synth in unison mode can sound like a monosynth with 12 oscillators. Many synths can produce two independent tone colors simultaneously. A few instruments feature multi-timbral voices, meaning that each voice can be programmed to produce an independent sound.

TRIGGERING SYSTEMS

When playing a synthesizer, your keyboard technique greatly affects your articulation and expression. When you play staccato, the envelope of each note may never reach the decay stage. If notes overlap when you play legato, holding down each key for the note's full duration, the result hinges on the design of the instrument.

The technique of playing a monophonic synthesizer, or a polysynth in unison mode, depends on how it's triggered. If it has a multiple-triggering system, a new Note On signal appears at the beginning of each new key depression, regardless of whether the previous note has been released. Each key you depress produces a complete envelope, cutting off the release stage of the previous envelope if necessary. With single-triggering, however, each key depression triggers a new envelope only if there's no gate; that is, if no other key is being held down. Single-triggering lets you play a legato phrase with only one prescribed attack at the beginning. Either triggering systems is useful in its own way. Some instruments offer a choice by featuring a trigger mode selection switch.

VOICE ASSIGNMENT

How you play a polyphonic keyboard depends on its voice assignment. The two most common voice assignment schemes are continuous and reset. In continuous mode, the voices are assigned in numerical order, that is, one after another. Once a particular voice is played, it won't play again until all

Multiple Triggering

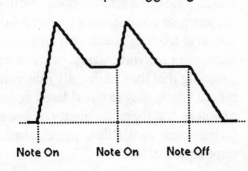

Note On   Note On   Note Off

Single Triggering

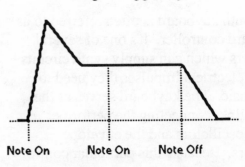

Note On   Note On   Note Off

the other voices have played in turn. If the first key you depress plays voice 1, then the second key plays voice 2, followed by 3, 4, and so on, until all the voices have been played. At that point, the cycle begins again at voice 1. For example, if you play a 3-note chord on a 6-voice synthesizer, and it plays voices 1, 2, and 3, then the next 3-note chord plays voices 4, 5, and 6. An 8-note arpeggio on the same keyboard, beginning with voice 1, uses voices 1, 2, 3, 4, 5, 6, 1, and 2, in that order. If the sound has a long release time, it might continue sounding until that particular voice is re-triggered several key depressions later. If a key is held down, and a voice is sustained, subsequent key depressions will cycle through the remaining voices. For example, if you have a 6-voice synth and your left hand holds down a 3-note chord which uses voices 1, 2, and 3, anything you play with your right hand will cycle through voices 4, 5, and 6.

The advantage of continuous voice assignment is that the release stage of every note can last until that voice is re-triggered, if desired. The envelope isn't cut off by the next key depression. With long envelopes, you can build up a 16-note chord on a 16-voice instrument, and you don't even need 16 fingers. One disadvantage of continuous voice assignment is that portamento is much more difficult to control.

If a keyboard adheres to the reset voice assignment mode, subsequent key depressions trigger the same voices continually. The lowest-numbered voices are always the first to play. When you play a single melody line without overlapping notes, voice 1 is played over and over again. Every time you release the keys, the next key depressed always sounds the first voice. When you play a series of 3-note chords, only voices 1, 2, and 3 are played. To hear the highest-numbered voice, the maximum number of keys must be depressed all at once. With reset voice assignment, a convincing monophonic line can be played on a polyphonic synthesizer. If you play a single melody line on a synth with continuous voice assignment, the note releases may overlap. Unless you can switch off individual channels, the only way to play a monophonic line which re-triggers the same voice is in unison mode, which triggers all voices with each key depression.

PRIORITY SYSTEMS

Because most synthesizers can produce only a limited number of simultaneous notes, a priority system is also required. It decides which notes will be heard if the number of keys depressed exceeds the number of available voices, and in what order. If too many keys are held down, keyboards with low-note priority will play only the lowest notes depressed. If you hold down the maximum number and press a higher key, nothing happens. If you depress a lower key, a voice is stolen from the highest key and is assigned to the new key. A high-note priority keyboard plays only the highest keys depressed, just the opposite of low-note priority. On some keyboards, once the maximum number of keys is down, additional key depressions are ignored. That's called first-note priority. With last-note priority, when you depress any key after the maximum number is down, the note which has been down the longest disappears and the new note takes its place.

SPLITS AND LAYERS

Many polyphonic keyboards feature a split mode. A voice or group of voices can be played on one part of the keyboard, perhaps the top half, and other voices can be played on the remainder. A split keyboard lets you play a funky bass patch with your left hand and strings with your right, for example. Some instruments let you dictate where the split occurs. One splitting scheme assigns a fixed number of voices to each part of the keyboard, say four voices to the left hand and two voices to the right, or the other way around. Other instruments feature dynamic voice assignment, which allocates voices to either side of the split point as needed, up to the maximum number available.

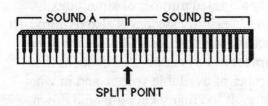

SPLIT POINT

Most synths which are capable of keyboard splits can also layer sounds by assigning two different voices to each key. A few keyboards may be split into many zones, each controlling a different tone color. When synthesizing natural-sounding timbres, a keyboard which can be split into zones lets you compensate for tonal differences in various instrumental registers. Multiple sounds may be layered by assigning them to the same zone. If zone locations are stored as patch parameters, this information is sometimes called a keyboard map.

TOUCH-SENSITIVE KEYBOARDS

Quite a few synthesizer keyboards are touch-sensitive. Like an acoustic piano, they respond to the dynamics of your playing style. Touch may control loudness or filter brightness, or it may affect envelope parameters, pitch, waveform, or vibrato depth or rate. Sometimes touch information is assignable to a number of sources, sometimes it isn't. A velocity-sensitive keyboard determines how quickly a key is struck and delivers a proportional control signal. It may also measure how quickly the key is released and change the envelope's release time. Recent professional synthesizers are almost always velocity-sensitive.

A force- or pressure-sensitive keyboard has sensors to determine how hard you press on a key after it's down. This is also called second touch or aftertouch. A few keyboards have polyphonic pressure-sensitivity, with a pressure sensor under each key, but most have monophonic pressure-sensitivity, with one sensor for the entire keyboard. Of course, a velocity or pressure signal affects only synthesizers designed to respond to touch-sensitivity.

OCTAVE SWITCHING

Some keyboards have an octave switch which lets you transpose the entire keyboard up or down exactly one octave, or possibly two. This feature really increases the range of the keyboard. A 3-octave keyboard doesn't have to be limited to just three octaves. Let's suppose that you're playing a blazing solo, and you run out of keys at the top of the keyboard. No problem. Simply hit the octave switch, drop your playing hand an octave, and continue ascending. Without octave switching, you may have to retune the oscillators to play in different registers.

ARPEGGIATORS

A number of instruments feature an arpeggiator function, which automatically plays arpeggios whenever two or more keys are depressed at the same time. When you play a chord, the notes are triggered in sequence, rather than all at once. The rate of arpeggiation is controlled by a clock signal, either from a low-frequency oscillator or synced to another instrument or circuit. A switch is often provided to govern the direction of the arpeggio, whether up, down, alternately up and down, in the order depressed, or in a random order. A few arpeggiators extend a chord over additional octaves. Some instruments memorize which keys are depressed and continue to play even when you remove your hand, a technique called latching.

Up Arpeggio

Down Arpeggio

Up and Down Arpeggio

CONTINUOUS CONTROLLERS

Continuous controllers are manual devices which produce a wide range of control values, such as pitch bend or modulation wheels. Most performers play the keyboard with their right hands as they work these two controllers with their left hands. Other continuous controllers include pedals, footswitches, and breath controllers. These devices are very important, because they're primarily used to impart expression to your playing. Pitch bend and modulation controllers are usually located just to the left of the keyboard itself. Left-hand controllers come in many forms: wheels, knobs, sliders, levers, joysticks, ribbons, or pressure-sensitive pads. Most people have a preference for one or the other. You may find that thumbwheels feel the most natural to you, but that's strictly a matter of personal taste and experience.

PITCH BEND AND MODULATION

Pitch bend lets you momentarily raise or lower any pitch by a desired amount. Many instrumental performers employ pitch bend. A guitarist bends a string by pushing it sideways against the fret board, or by pressing a bar attached to the bridge, which varies the tension on the strings. A sax player can bend notes by applying pressure to the reed. A violinist bends pitch by just sliding his or her finger up or down the fingerboard. A synthesist uses the pitch bend controller.

A pitch bend controller changes either the keyboard signal governing pitch, or the oscillator frequency directly. Push it up, and the frequency increases. Push it down, and the frequency drops. The range of pitch bend varies from one model to the next, and can sometimes be switched or programmed to the desired maximum interval. On many instruments, it's quite possible to bend pitch by turning the master tuning pot. It's much easier to use the pitch bender, because when you return the controller to its initial position, it always puts the pitch right back where it started. Pitch bend makes it possible to change the frequencies of multiple oscillators on multiple instruments at the same time and to an equal degree.

The modulation controller is a specialized attenuator which governs the depth or amount that a given parameter is modulated. Its function depends on which control signal it attenuates and its destination. The modulation controller usually affects the depth of LFO modulation on oscillator frequency, and sometimes pulse width or filter frequency. It is most often used to vary vibrato depth as you play. Its mastery is a skill you should acquire if you want to make the most of your synthesizer's expressive capabilities.

OPTIONAL CONTROLLERS

Some synthesizers feature an optional breath controller, a small mouthpiece for controlling LFO modulation or envelope parameters with breath pressure. The depth of its control signal depends on how hard you blow into it. This controller can be indispensable in synthesizing brass, wood-wind, and vocal sounds.

Often, foot controllers are included with a new synth, or they can be purchased as optional accessories. A footswitch may be used to shift octaves, hold a note or chord, start and stop a sequencer, turn the porta-mento on and off, step through a series of patch programs, or extend release time, like a piano sustain pedal. At least one synth features a switch you can tap with your foot to manually determine the sequencer's metronome rate.

Pedals are extremely handy control devices, because they free your hands for playing the keyboard. An active synth pedal generates a control signal that's proportional to the angle of the treadle. Its function depends on how it's assigned. If your synth has the appropriate inputs, this signal may alter parameters such as filter frequency, vibrato depth or rate, pitch bend, volume, or glide rate.

PORTAMENTO

Most synthesizers feature glide or portamento. A portamento circuit lets you slide smoothly from one note or chord to the next, like a steel guitar or a slide trombone. When the portamento is on, there's a lag in the time it takes to change from one pitch to another. The glide time is usually controlled by a manual pot. Some synths have a porta-mento rate that varies with the width of the interval. When it's set for one octave per second, it takes half a second to glide half an octave, and three seconds to glide three octaves. Another type of portamento takes the same period of time no matter what the interval, as long as the position of the porta-mento pot is unchanged. If it takes one second to glide up a semitone, its also takes one second to glide two octaves. Each type of portamento has a characteristic sound, but very few instruments give you a choice. Portamento can substitute for pitch bend by presetting its depth and turning it on and off at the proper moments.

Some synths feature automatic porta-mento when playing monophonically, also called autoglide or fingered portamento, so that the portamento is activated only when you depress a key while still holding the previous key. Glissando (gliss), also called quantized portamento, is similar to regular portamento, but pitch changes in discrete semitonal steps. Glissando permits fast chromatic runs which might not be possible by hand.

MIDI

Once upon a time, all synthesizers were modular. They had keyboards, oscillators, filters, and other specialized circuits contained in separate, voltage-controlled modules, interconnected by patchcords. Later synthesizers were self-contained and much less flexible. A few could share information with outboard sequencers which were specifically designed to interface with instruments from the same manufacturer.

Recent electronic instruments incorporate an interface called MIDI, which stands for Musical Instrument Digital Interface. MIDI makes it possible to link together synthesizers, microcomputers, sequencers, drum machines, and signal processors, forming a new kind of modular system.

Throughout the history of electronic music, musicians have wanted to connect multiple instruments together to create a whole greater than the sum of its parts. The greatest stumbling block was that instruments from one company were incompatible with instruments from another. In late 1982, several major American and Japanese synthesizer manufacturers agreed on MIDI as a standard communications protocol for controlling several instruments with a single keyboard or with a personal computer. Ever since the final MIDI specification was adopted in August 1983, most musicians won't buy electronic instruments that don't feature MIDI, so manufacturers have been forced to implement at least part of the MIDI standard on every new product they make.

Virtually all modern electronic musical gear is microprocessor-based. All information generated within each instrument is in the form of a digital code. Establishing a standard was simply a matter of getting enough people to make their codes at least partially compatible, which isn't as easy as it sounds. Synthesizers use a lot of diverse hardware and they're all programmed differently. MIDI provides a common language for communication among instruments, making it possible to build an integrated network for recording and performance. MIDI doesn't actually encode the music itself, but performance parameters — keyboard depressions, patch changes, operating modes, and so on — are communicated within a system.

One advantage of MIDI's modular concept is that you can pick and choose system components which best suit your individual needs, very much like putting together a stereo system. Your favorite keyboard, which may be a self-contained, independent controller, can be linked to any MIDI instrument you please. To add additional synthesizers, you don't necessarily need more keyboards. A synthesizer expander module will suffice, saving space and money. If you want to add a computer to the network, you have several choices, and an even greater number of choices when choosing software to control the system.

WHAT CAN YOU DO WITH MIDI?

At its most basic level, MIDI lets the user tie in one synthesizer with another so that both can be played from the same keyboard. One is the transmitter, generating information which is understood by the second synth, the receiver. For instance, when you play on Synth A's keyboard, the sound of Synth B can be layered along with Synth A. It may also be possible to bend pitch or change program numbers and have both instruments respond. When you recall program number 64 on Synth A, for example, Synth B also switches to its program number 64. Usually, this feature may be turned on and off at will. This allows patches with twice the thickness, twice the complexity, and twice the power of one synthesizer alone. Most instruments are capable of both transmitting and receiving MIDI signals.

stored in Synth B's memory. Individual parameter changes made on one can alter the sound of the other.

Many synthesizers are equipped with on-board sequencers, but these sequencers may not be capable of recording keyboard velocity and pressure data, program changes, tempo changes, and other aspects of a recorded performance, or they may not be capable of overdubbing tracks. A separate sequencer may be required to run the whole show. Such a sequencer can take the place of a tape recorder with digital memory replacing the tape. A full-blown MIDI system might incorporate a multitrack sequencer which records all the mechanics of your keyboard performance. When you've laid down a number of tracks, the sequencer can control one or more synthesizers, playing back a fully-orchestrated version of what's been recorded, complete with independent programmed patch changes, pitch bends,

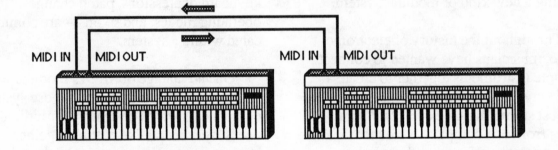

If the instruments are from different manufacturers, it's unlikely that parameter information is processed in exactly the same way (at present), so most parameter changes on one may not affect the other. Every synthesizer controls a subset of all possible parameters. But if the two units are of the same make and model, it may be possible to transfer complete patch programs from Synth A to the Synth B, which can then be

and other performance details. A drum machine can be synchronized to the sequencer, and signal processors equipped with MIDI can switch from one pre-programmed effect to another. You can imagine how such a system might be useful onstage or in the studio. One performer can sound like a whole band. Entire compositions can be arranged in advance and recorded to tape in one take.

MIDI makes it possible to sync almost any drum machine to almost any sequencer, or any sequencer to any drum machine. A MIDI clock signal from the drum machine can control the playback tempo of a synthesizer's internal sequencer, or even its arpeggiator, so that arpeggios and recorded sequences will play in perfect time with the percussion sequence. Some MIDI-equipped drum machines can be programmed from the keyboard in real time, with each key representing a different drum sound. Some units even respond to touch-sensitivity, allowing the programming of dynamics in a percussion track.

Signal processors are now being made MIDI-compatible to expand your networking capabilities even more. Effects parameters stored in a signal processing device's memory are recalled by program numbers, just like synthesizer patches. In a MIDIfied digital delay, each program may have a different preset effect such as chorus, flanging, doubling, looping, or discrete echo. When a patch program is recalled on the master synth, an accompanying effect which may be an integral part of that particular sound is also recalled.

A synthesist's life is greatly enhanced by using a personal computer to compose, perform, and record music. Computer manufacturers and software developers were slower than instrument makers to respond to the pleas of the MIDI-hungry masses at first, but droves of them finally jumped on the bandwagon. MIDI interfaces are available for computers from Apple, IBM, Commodore, Atari, and other major brands. Some MIDI software lets you use the computer as a sequencer, and some lets you transcribe music simply by playing it.

Another type of software lets you design and store hundreds of patch programs on a single disk for quick recall. There are comprehensive music processing programs that combine functions. You can record and arrange your performance in either real time or step time, edit your work, then print out a hard copy of your completed score, all within the same application.

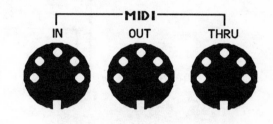

HARDWARE

The MIDI spec is a document published by the International MIDI Association. It specifies the hardware and transmission requirements, the MIDI data format, channel modes, and command messages. Not every instrument is programmed to understand the entire MIDI specification.

To keep the expense down, there's very little hardware involved. Every MIDI connection is made by a shielded, twisted pair cable with a 5-pin DIN plug at each end. Only three pins are actually used. Conductors are connected to pins 4 and 5, with the shield attached to pin 2. Alternately, XLR connectors may be used for road-resistant applications. Cables should not exceed 50 feet in length. Two cables are necessary for two-way communication between instruments. Each MIDI instrument has at least two serial ports. These are DIN (or XLR) jacks labeled MIDI In and MIDI Out. An optional port is labeled MIDI Thru. MIDI

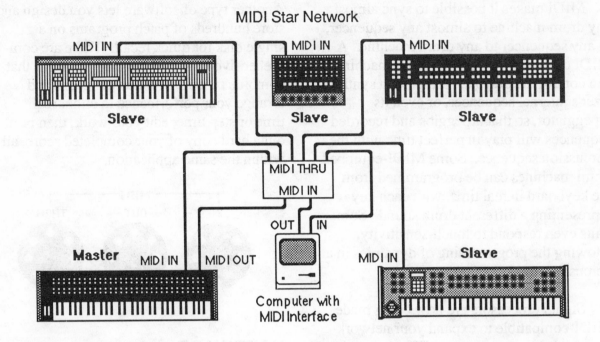

MIDI Star Network

In receives MIDI-encoded information, and MIDI Out transmits it. MIDI Thru transmits exactly what it receives through its MIDI In port. If the signal at MIDI Out duplicated MIDI In, data would be trapped in a perpetual loop, so the Thru port is necessary. The MIDI In jack is optoisolated to prevent noise and ground loops. Transmission speed is 31.25 kBaud, or 31,250 bits per second.

SYSTEM CONFIGURATIONS

There are at least two ways to set up a MIDI network: as a daisy chain or as a star network. A system with MIDI cables running from a master instrument to slave instruments in series is called a daisy chain. Typically, a cable goes from the Master's MIDI Out to Slave A's MIDI In, then another cable goes from Slave A's MIDI Thru to Slave B's MIDI In, and so on. When you play the master keyboard, all the slaves

may play as well. Notes played on Slave A only affect that instrument, instead of transmitting information to subsequent instruments, because they're not connected to Slave A's MIDI Out.

One of MIDI's limitations is that daisy chaining becomes impractical with more than four instruments. 31.25 kBaud is pretty fast, but because MIDI is a asynchronous serial interface, information can get backed up, causing perceptible time delays when you exceed the recommended four-instrument maximum in a daisy chain. In a serial interface, information flows in single file, one bit after another. Parallel interfaces pass larger amounts of information through multiple pin connections simultaneously. Parallel interfaces may be capable of transferring data much faster, but the hardware itself is more expensive. Some manufacturers install their own proprietary parallel interfaces in addition to MIDI, but this adds to the cost of each instrument.

To use more than four instruments in a system requires a configuration called a star network. For a star network, you need a box with a MIDI In port and multiple MIDI Thru ports. MIDI Thru boxes are available from various manufacturers. All slaves are connected to the master through the box. The number of instruments in a star network is limited only by the number of MIDI Thru ports available.

CHANNELS AND MODES

Transmission and reception of musical information is divided into 16 channels. Don't confuse channels with voices — every channel can be polyphonic, and the number of voices is only limited by the instruments in the system. Channel selection messages address different information to individual instruments or voices. For example, a split keyboard can direct its left-hand note data to an instrument assigned to one channel and right-hand data to another instrument on another channel.

All 16 channels are transmitted in series over the same wire. Most instruments and computer software let you select on which channels information is sent and received, much as you select television channels. A television receives all channels using a

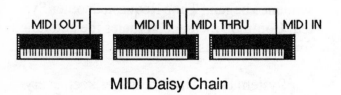

MIDI Daisy Chain

common antenna or cable hook-up. You can connect as many televisions tuned to as many channels as you like to the same antenna without degrading the signal. Like a television antenna, a single MIDI cable can handle all the information carried on every channel. Almost any number of instruments can be connected to each channel. Unlike a single television, however, one instrument can receive data on all channels simultaneously. Unfortunately, a few instruments aren't capable of channel selection and always receive and transmit on Channel 1. The best way to find out how your synth deals with channels is to read the manual.

MIDI messages also select the operating modes of each instrument within the system. These modes determine how channels are assigned and whether each channel is monophonic or polyphonic. Almost every synthesizer model has its own method for selecting modes. Again, consult your manual.

There are three mode messages: Omni, Poly, and Mono. Most instruments power up in Omni mode when they're turned on, receiving messages transmitted on any and all channels. Messages are transmitted on a single basic channel, usually channel 1. When Omni is turned off, the receiver accepts messages only on its assigned channel. Mono mode allows only one voice per channel, and Poly allows normal polyphonic voice assignment. There are four possible combinations of these three mode messages, resulting in four MIDI modes: Omni On/Poly, Omni On/Mono, Omni Off/Poly, and Omni Off/Mono.

Omni On/Poly, also called Omni mode or Mode 1, makes all instruments in a system accept polyphonic messages transmitted on any channel. When you play the master keyboard in this mode, all synthesizers in the system respond. If both Omni and Mono are on (Mode 2), all instruments in the system play the same thing no matter what channel they're assigned, but they're each limited to one voice. All other voices are turned off. When Omni is turned off in Poly mode (Mode 3), an instrument receives polyphonic messages on its assigned channel only. That way, you can assign one polysynth to Channel 1, another to Channel 2, and so on, and they can still play more than one voice at a time. For multiple synthesizers under sequencer control, Omni Off/Poly is your best bet. If Omni is off and Mono is on (Mode 4), each channel controls one voice only. Unless your synthesizer is multi-timbral, this mode turns it into a monophonic instrument. Multi-timbral instruments can assign a MIDI channel to each voice.

MIDI MESSAGES

MIDI includes a digital language which communicates by specific commands. Messages concerning particular voices and modes are encoded with channel numbers. Others are intended for the entire system.

Whenever you play a note on a MIDI instrument, it produces a Note On command. Note On events and associated velocity data can be assigned to specific channels. Note Off events are also channel-assignable. Key pressure data may be for individual notes or for all voices assigned to a given channel. When a note is played on the master instrument, a message is transmitted that tells the slave that a note is on, its pitch, and its attack velocity. When the note ends, another message indicates that the note is off, its pitch, and the release velocity. Of course, velocity data is ignored by instruments that aren't designed to respond to it.

Program changes are assignable to specific channels. Individual channels can also respond to information from continuous controllers, such as joysticks or foot-pedals, used for pitch bend, modulation, and the like. The MIDI specification allows for up to 128 differrent continuous controllers, each assigned a number. Synth makers have only recently agreed on standards of how one instrument might react to a continuous controller from another manufacturer's instrument. With older MIDI synths, bending up half a step on the master synthesizer may raise the pitch a whole step on another instrument, or one instrument's breath controller may have the same number as another's LFO rate control.

MIDI commands which aren't channel-assignable are divided into three types: System Common messages, System Real Time messages, and System Exclusive messages. System Common messages include Song Select, which chooses one of 128 sequences by its assigned number, and a Song Position Pointer, which indicates the number of MIDI clock beats since the sequence began. Tune Request, another System Common message, initiates the autotune function of all instruments which support it.

System Real Time messages keep everything in perfect synchronization. These include a timing clock, along with the commands Start, Stop, and Continue. When the Play command is initiated, a sequence begins from its first measure at a tempo determined by the master clock. The standard MIDI clock rate is 24 steps per beat. A sequence can be stopped on any beat by the Stop command, and continued from that point by the Continue command. Other System Real Time messages include an already obsolete Active Sensing command, which turns off all voices if transmission ceases, and System Reset, which returns all instruments to their power-up conditions.

System Exclusive messages are recognized by instruments from individual manufacturers. Each manufacturer is assigned a System Exclusive identification number. This type of message is ignored by instruments which don't recognize the ID code. It's up to the instrument maker to decide what functions, if any, are System Exclusive, allowing voice editing by computer, for instance, or the exchange of parameter information by two or more identical instruments. A command at the end of a System Exclusive message terminates System Exclusive status.

PROBLEMS AND PROMISES

Like any struggling standard, MIDI has its problems and limitations. Not all "MIDI-compatible" devices are completely compatible. At present, the majority of MIDI instruments don't implement the whole specification, just the most critical portions. In response to consumer demand, some manufacturers have tried to retrofit their old designs with MIDI with varying degrees of success. Not everyone is pleased with the specification as it stands, saying the rigidly-defined spec limits the development of new synthesizer technology. Others complain that the transmission rate needs to be faster than 31.25 kBaud (which isn't exactly slow) for complex, multiple instrument setups. When many channels are in use, the processing of MIDI information can result in perceptible delays. Because it flows in a serial stream, data can get backed up. When backed-up data exceeds buffer limits, it's lost.

After decades of electronic music, most people are thankful to have a standard at all. MIDI opens up many wonderful possibilities which didn't exist before. In its full implementation, it does everything it's supposed to do. As long as MIDI is with us, newly-developed instruments will be at least partially compatible with old ones. Obsolescence and depreciation will hopefully be diminished by its existance.

MIDI is, however, a constantly evolving standard. Members of the MIDI Manufacturer's Association regularly meet to iron out the details of its implementation, insuring greater compatibility among MIDI instruments and devices. New uses for MIDI are an open possibility. You can expect MIDI software that no one's even imagined yet. There's talk of a future MIDI spec which uses all five DIN pins, but if such changes are ever agreed upon, it will almost certainly support older MIDI instruments. Not very long ago, getting synthesizer makers to agree on anything was nearly impossible. Now that they've accepted MIDI, it's unlikely that they'll agree to change it drastically for quite some time.

OTHER INTERFACES

SYNC

In addition to MIDI, there are numerous other schemes for interconnecting electronic musical equipment. Most of these methods let you play sequencers and drum machines in synchronization with one another or with taped performances, by transmitting and receiving audible pulses from a computer-generated clock. The clock serves as a metronome for controlling rhythm. Some methods of sync have advantages over MIDI, others have disadvantages, and some are useful in tandem with MIDI. With some types, you can record the sync signal on one track of a multitrack tape recorder, then record additional tracks in perfect time with the prerecorded sync track.

Many drum machines use a clock sync in which each beat, usually defined as a quarter note's duration, is divided into a number of pulses. The number of pulses per quarter note, referred to as the clock frequency, depends on exactly what brand of instrument is producing and reading the sync signal. Many manufacturers have their own "standards" for pulse division. Usually, the clock frequency is divisible by both three and four, which allows for quantizing duplets, triplets, and quadruplets. The higher the clock rate, the greater the degree of rhythmic resolution. A lot of Roland, Korg, and E-mu equipment syncs to a rate of 24 pulses per quarter note. The LinnDrum syncs to 48 pulses per beat. The Oberheim System sends and reads 96 per beat, and Fairlight uses a high-res standard of 192 clocks per beat. You can buy sync boxes from companies like J. L. Cooper, Garfield, and Roland, which match the clock rates of different makes of equipment by multiplying or dividing their frequencies.

Instruments from various companies may also vary in sync signal frequency, level (threshold), and polarity. Sync signal frequency may be anywhere from 150 Hz to 1200 Hz. Polarity depends on whether the instrument syncs to the positive (rising) edge or negative (falling) edge of the pulse signal. A few instruments and devices let you configure the sync inputs and outputs to accept and generate almost any type of clock signal.

Most sequencers and drum machines start and stop whenever the sync signal begins and ends. Some non-MIDI Roland gear produces and requires an additional start/stop signal to respond to an external clock. When a Roland unit is being driven by an external master clock, its run/stop button is disabled. A few sync boxes supply the extra signal needed by these instruments.

Clock sync is best suited to live applications. Problems may arise, however, when you record clock signals on tape. Sync pulses are often too weak to record accurately, resulting in distortion of the sync waveform. If dropout occurs on the tape, part of the sync track is irretrievably lost. Other methods seek to eliminate the problems of synchronized recording.

FSK

Another important sync signal is called FSK, short for frequency shift keying. FSK alternates two audible tones at the rate of the clock frequency. Roland and Oberheim both use FSK in some instruments, but because their clock rates and FSK frequencies differ, the units are incompatible. Since FSK is an audible signal (unlike MIDI clock), it can be recorded on tape. Once recorded, synchronized overdubs are almost easy. Some MIDI computer interfaces and MIDI boxes incorporate parallel FSK generators for syncing MIDI instruments to tape.

A distinct disadvantage of FSK is that it doesn't indicate beat or measure numbers, so there's no way to find your location in a sequence. You can't rewind or fast forward the tape to the part you want to dub over. You always have to start at the beginning.

SMPTE

A few newer instruments, sequencers, and interface devices incorporate SMPTE time code, which comes to us from the Society of Motion Picture and Television Engineers. Since 1967, it has been used to synchronize audio to film and videotape. SMPTE divides hours into minutes, minutes into seconds, seconds into frames, and frames into subframes. Though frame rates vary, the standard division for American film is 30 frames per second. Recording studios use SMPTE code for syncing multitrack tape machines together. By syncing two 24-track machines to a common SMPTE reader/generator, you can record up to 46 tracks (48 tracks minus two tracks for time code) in sync.

One major advantage of using SMPTE sync in electronic music is that it remembers the location of every note and measure in a sequence. A sequencer can be instructed to go to the start of any measure and proceed from there. SMPTE lets a multitrack sequencer operate more like a multitrack tape deck. Some devices, like the Roland SBX-80 Sync Box, generate and read SMPTE code as well as MIDI clock. A few instruments, including the Emulator II, Synclavier, and Fairlight CMI, offer a SMPTE clock for syncing to tape. The less expensive route to SMPTE sync is using a MIDI computer interface which generates and reads SMPTE signals.

INTERFACING OLDER INSTRUMENTS

Most synthesizers made since the early Seventies have some sort of interfacing capabilities. Believe it or not, there were pre-digital developments for controlling two or more compatible synthesizers with a single keyboard. Many older synthesizers have input and output jacks for control voltage, gate, and trigger signals. Using patchcords, these signals can be routed to or from another instrument's corresponding jacks for layering sounds. The old Oberheim Expander Module (SEM) was specifically designed to interface to a number of popular synthesizers to supplement their voices. The Roland MC202 synth/sequencer, among others, records and transmits control voltages and gates which can be applied to instruments from other companies. Even the newer Oberheim Xpander accepts control voltages and gates from keyboards and sequencers which supply such signals. The longevity of older instruments can be preserved by using MIDI boxes which convert control voltages and gates to MIDI code and vice versa.

A few older instruments have proprietary digital interfaces, allowing them to be linked to instruments and devices built by the same company. The Oberheim System, for example, consists of an OBXa, OB-SX, or OB-8 synthesizer, a DSX sequencer, and a DMX or DX drum machine. Some Roland instruments feature their DCG (Digital Communication Bus) interface. A few makes, including Chroma and PPG, still feature proprietary interfaces in addition to MIDI. For some pre-MIDI instruments, adapters are available to convert signals from their proprietary interfaces to MIDI signals.

Several older synthesizers feature an external audio input jack for processing audio signals from a different instrument or from other sound sources. The Minimoog, ARP Odyssey, and Oberheim modular synthesizers all have audio inputs on their back panels. The Sequential Circuits Pro-One even generates a gate when it detects a signal level above a certain threshold, triggering an envelope for each new sound event. A few modular instruments have envelope followers, which duplicate the envelopes of audio input signals. The Korg MS-20 has an external signal processor which includes a pitch-to-voltage convertor and an envelope follower. The practical usefulness of processing audio signals with synthesizers is rather limited, so external audio inputs have largely faded into history.

SEQUENCERS

Modern sequencers are specialized digital recorders which can play synthesizers automatically. Most of them memorize anything you play, then play it right back at you. Performance information is stored in the sequencer's digital memory to be recalled at the touch of a button. In live performance, a sequencer gives you extra hands. To the composer, a sequencer is an indispensable tool for hearing melodic, harmonic, rhythmic, and timbral combinations without the aid of other musicians. In the studio, a sequencer lets you work out entire arrangements before the tape starts rolling. Other musicians can preview their individual parts in advance, played by one or more synthesizers under sequencer control.

Just about every sequencer sold today is designed to control MIDI instruments. Until the advent of MIDI, digital sequencers were mostly outboard devices for controlling a particular instrument or system. These pioneering devices include the Oberheim

DSX, Sequential 1005 Poly-Sequencer, and Roland CSQ sequencers. A few sequencers, like the Roland MicroComposers, can control a variety of synthesizers with standard control voltage and gate inputs. Fortunately, MIDI gives us a universal way of doing things.

There are many types of MIDI sequencers. Some synthesizers have on-board sequencers included in their design, using their built-in microprocessors and memory to record and store performance data. Often, sequences can be dumped to and from tape, just like patch programs. Many synth sequencers record only what's played on their keyboards, but others record from any MIDI source, even from another sequencer. Dedicated sequencers, such as the Yamaha QX-1, Korg SQD-1, and Casio SZ-1, are self-contained modules which can be used with almost any MIDI synthesizer. They usually have a larger amount of accessible memory than on-board sequencers, so

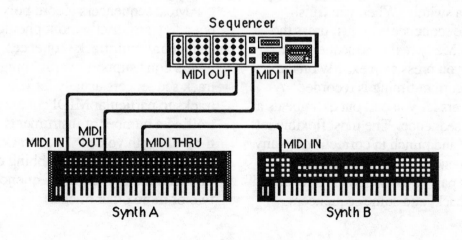

they're capable of storing longer sequences or a greater number of tracks. They're portable and simple to operate, but upgrading to the latest version or adding more memory can be expensive. Then there's MIDI software which turns a personal computer with a MIDI interface into a sequencer. A computer-based sequencer often has the advantage of a more powerful microprocessor and greater memory at a reasonable cost. With a portable computer, you can use whatever sequencer program best suits your needs in any situation, and upgrade it for much less expense.

SEQUENCE RECORDING

There are at least two methods of entering music into a sequencer: real time and step time. Some sequencers let you choose either method, but many feature only one or the other. The real time method usually incorporates the audible click of an electronic metronome to keep the beat as you record. Many real time sequencers don't begin recording until you play the first note. If you want the first measure to begin with a rest, there must be some way of starting the recording other than playing a key, usually by pressing a switch. When you finish recording the sequence, you just press the stop button. Many real time sequencers require that you press stop exactly on the beat so that correct timing is recorded. A few sequencers let you edit out extra beats at the end of a sequence. The most flexible let you go back and punch in corrections to any track or sequence. Tempo can be programmed as part of the sequence or changed during playback, and some sequencers remember tempo changes made during recording. A finished sequence may be assigned a name or number, then sequence data can be dumped to disk or cassette for more permanent storage.

Some real time sequencers feature auto-correction, which "rounds off" each note to the nearest 16th note, for example. A few let you specify the degree of resolution, dividing each beat into fractions. Notes may be quantized to the nearest 96th of a beat, or 48th or a beat, or whatever. Sometimes you can indicate that Note Off messages will occur exactly on the fraction of a beat, as well as Note On commands. Auto-correction is most often used to clean up an uneven performance.

A step time sequencer lets you record one note or chord at a time. On playback, all notes are quantized into mathematically precise divisions. There's usually some provision for indicating a rest instead of a note, like pressing a switch. The simplest step-loaded digital sequencers can only play notes and rests of equal duration, but most have the means to tie notes together, creating longer notes and rests.

Most sequencers record polyphonically, but a few are strictly monophonic. Some can record multitrack sequences, while others don't support overdubbing. Multitrack sequencers usually let you assign tracks to particular MIDI channels for controlling a number of instruments or multi-timbral synth voices. Each track is polyphonic, and may allow dubbing over what's on that track or merging sequences from two or more other tracks.

Sequencers are limited in the number of notes or MIDI events they can record by the amount of available memory. Some of them let you filter out unnecessary MIDI commands to conserve memory and to avoid commands which may confuse instruments which aren't designed to recognize them.

Sequencing is playing an increasingly large part in producing music. Sequencers may not be for everybody, but they cost a great deal less than comparable multitrack tape machines, and both floppy disks and cassettes are cheaper than reels of multitrack recording tape. You still need tape (at least, most of us do) for recording acoustic and electro-acoustic instruments and voices, but that will certainly change as digital recording equipment becomes more accessible. In the meantime, MIDI keyboard recorders are flexible, they're affordable, and they get the job done.

Programming Techniques

BASIC TECHNIQUES

TUNING

To play with other instruments, your synthesizer should probably be tuned to standard pitch (A-440). Most analog or hybrid synthesizers require a period of warming up before the VCOs stabilize, or their frequencies may drift slightly. If your synth has automatic tuning, just press the appropriate switch, wait a few seconds, and you're all tuned up. Depending on the instrument, you may have to adjust the master tune control as well. If your synth is totally analog, just follow these instructions:

Turn the oscillator tuning controls to approximately center. If there's a range selection pot, turn it to its middle range (8'). Switch the keyboard to its middle octave and depress A above middle C. Find a reliable pitch source — piano, guitar, tuning fork, anything you can trust to be in tune — and play an A above middle C. (If your synth has an internal A-440 pitch reference, that will do nicely.) Adjust oscillator 1's frequency pots or the master tuning pot until the pitch closely matches your reference pitch. Raise or lower the octave, if necessary.

Carefully adjust the fine tuning pot (if there is one) to match the pitches exactly. As the pitch approaches the reference pitch in frequency, you may hear a pronounced pulsation as each sound alternately cancels and reinforces the other. Whenever two audio signals of nearly the same frequency or closely related frequencies are sounded together, they produce a low-frequency sideband, called beating, equal to the difference between the two signals. If you hear one beat per second, they're 1 Hz apart. Barely turn the fine tuning control until no beats can be detected. If you have additional audio oscillators, tune them by the same method, using oscillator 1 as a reference.

Many sounds require that the oscillators are slightly out of tune with one another. Deliberately detuning the oscillators thickens the sound, sometimes creating the illusion of multiple instruments. Oscillator 2 can be detuned 1 Hz or less, causing a beat every second or more. Most often the oscillators are just a few cents apart. (A cent is 1% of a semitone. A semitone, or half step, is the interval between two adjacent keys.)

You don't always want to tune the oscillators in unison, but it's a logical place to start. Some sounds demand tuning to other intervals. Raise the frequency of oscillator 2 until its pitch is exactly one octave above oscillator 1. As their frequencies converge, the beating will be less pronounced than with unison tuning, but it'll be there. Tune as precisely as you can.

Just for practice, now tune the second oscillator a perfect 5th above the first. Play a few notes and listen. Switch on the oscillator sync and play some more. Switch the sync back off and try other intervals, like a perfect 4th, major and minor 3rd, and larger intervals like a perfect 12th. Feel free to experiment with different tunings.

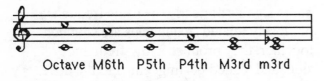

Octave M6th P5th P4th M3rd m3rd

THE NATURAL HARMONIC SERIES

Pythagoras, an ancient Greek mathematician, was the first to discover a mathematical relationship among the component frequencies of musical sounds. Your synthesizer can be used to demonstrate his discovery, the natural harmonic series. You might also gain some insight into how certain electronic effects are achieved.

First of all, turn your synthesizer's filter cutoff frequency and resonance up about halfway. Patch a single sawtooth wave through it. Play any low note, and give it a long release time. Then, very slowly, turn down the filter frequency. Listen as the filter emphasizes whatever harmonic is closest to the changing cutoff frequency. Vary the resonance setting for the greatest emphasis, just short of self-oscillation.

Now close the filter completely. Turn its frequency up just enough to pass the second harmonic, then the third, and so on, until you've swept the entire audible harmonic series. Repeat this procedure with various pulse waves.

If you have a DX synthesizer, turn on the Voice Initialize function. Find the Oscillator switches and press Frequency Coarse, which displays the frequency ratio "F COARSE= 1.00". Any note you play produces a simple sine wave at its fundamental frequency. As you slowly push the data slider up, you hear the harmonic series in succession, all the way up to the 31st harmonic. You can achieve the same results if you start with 1.00 and press the +1 data entry switch thirty times. Decreasing the frequency ratio steps down through the harmonic series.

PITCH BEND

Find your pitch bend controller, probably to the left of the keyboard. Pitch benders come in many forms, but they all move up and down (or sideways) from a center point. Some are spring-loaded so they return to center when released, and most have a center detent so you can feel the center position. If it's a knob, turn it clockwise to bend up and counterclockwise to bend down. If the pitch bender is a wheel, place your fingers over the synthesizer's left side and roll the wheel forward and back with your thumb. If it's a ribbon, press it anywhere with one finger and slide it up and down. Levers are either pushed away from you for bending down and pulled toward you for bending up, or just the opposite, or to the right for up and the left for down, depending on the model. You should have no trouble sorting it out.

Effective pitch bending is a technique worth learning and practicing. The styles of many well-known performers are recognized by the way they bend pitch. One of the best ways to perfect your pitch bending is to copy the licks of instrumental soloists. Listen to rock and blues guitarists, violinists, and sax players, as well as other synthesists.

Let's try an example of pitch bending. Guitarists sometimes bend from the minor 7th to the tonic of the key they're playing. There are at least two ways this can be done on a synthesizer: a) Push the pitch bend down a whole step before striking the tonic key, then bend up to center pitch before releasing the key; or, b) Strike the 7th key, bend up a whole step to the tonic, then quickly release the key and return the pitch bend to center just before you strike the tonic key. You actually depress two keys in succession with this second method. Either way, you have to think ahead.

It takes practice to learn to bend up or down by precise intervals. Most bends involve changing the pitch by a semitone or a whole step, so concentrate on getting those right at first. Later, work on larger intervals, like bending down a 4th or up a 5th.

With sufficient skill, you may be able to manually produce vibrato with the pitch bender. You must develop a keen ear and an accurate left hand to acquire a fluid bending style. When pitch bending comes naturally, you can play what you feel.

PULSE WIDTH MODULATION

Every pulse width has its own characteristic sound, because each has a unique harmonic structure. Thus a variety of basic timbres is possible from a variable pulse width oscillator. Alas, not every synthesizer features variable pulse width. A few allow you to switch between two or three preset duty cycles, but some only offer square waves. You get what you pay for.

Most synthesizers allow oscillator pulse width modulation from the LFO and from an envelope generator. As the modulating input changes, so does the width, and consequently, the spectrum of the modulated waveform. Let's take a look.

THE EFFECT OF AN LFO ON PULSE WIDTH

Modulated Oscillator Pulse Wave

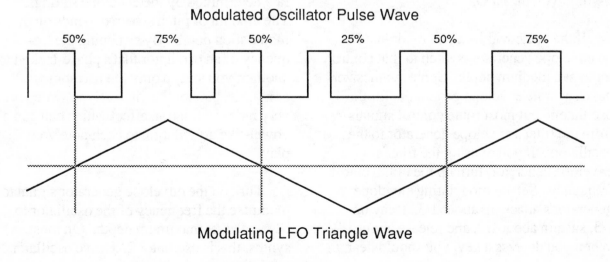

Modulating LFO Triangle Wave

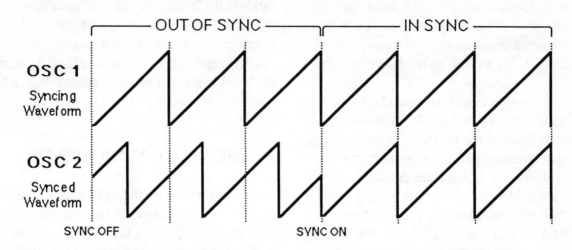

OUT OF SYNC   IN SYNC

OSC 1
Syncing
Waveform

OSC 2
Synced
Waveform

SYNC OFF   SYNC ON

The Effect of Oscillator Sync On Two Sawtooth Waves

Select a 50% pulse wave. Apply pulse width modulation (PWM) to the oscillator from the LFO, with the LFO generating a sine or triangle wave. Hold down some keys. When you increase the PWM depth, the duty cycle varies with each cycle of the LFO. Now turn the LFO frequency down to about .2 Hz (one cycle every five seconds), if you can. The result is a dramatic sweeping of harmonics that sounds a bit like slow phasing or chorusing. If the pulse width sweeps below zero or beyond 100%, the entire waveform is momentarily canceled in rhythm with the LFO.

If the pulse width can be modulated by an envelope generator, switch to that control input at a medium depth. Some synthesizers have separate envelope generators for the oscillators, but most route control signals from the filter's envelope generator to the oscillators. If you're using the filter's envelope generator, turn up the initial cutoff frequency. Set the modulating envelope generator's attack up about 1/3, decay up 1/3, sustain about 1/2, and release about 1/2. When you depress a key, you should hear an

obvious shift in harmonic structure. (To hear the full release stage, the amplifier must have a longer release time than the modulating envelope.) Continue to experiment with the envelope and initial pulse width settings to find sounds which may be useful.

SYNC SWEEP

Oscillator frequency can often be modulated by an envelope generator. With each key depression, the pitch rises and falls at a rate determined by the envelope settings. The amount of pitch sweep depends on the modulation depth. By sweeping the frequency of an oscillator that's phase-locked to another, you sweep only the harmonic emphasis, but not the pitch. Sync sweep is a very nice modulation effect which can add a vowel-like articulation to each note you play.

Turn on the envelope generator signal to modulate the frequency of the oscillator to be synced, at maximum depth. On most synths, this is oscillator 2. Leave oscillator 1 turned off. Adjust all envelope controls to their halfway positions. When you strike a key, the pitch is swept by the envelope generator. Now switch on the oscillator sync. When you strike another key, the pitch remains stable, but its harmonic content shifts. (Again, the amplifier release must be long enough to hear the final stage.)

CROSS-MODULATION

A type of frequency modulation, called cross-modulation or x-mod, occurs when one audio oscillator modulates the frequency of another. The resulting timbre contains a complex multitude of sidebands. Unlike ring modulation (a type of amplitude modulation), the original oscillator signals aren't suppressed. If the two oscillators are tuned together, the sidebands are harmonically related, producing a warm distortion of the modulated waveform. This technique can put more bite into your sound. If the oscillator frequencies aren't harmonically related, the timbre is an extremely dense, thick texture, overflowing with non-harmonic overtones. With the appropriate frequency ratios, you can use cross-modulation to synthesize metallic and bell-like timbres.

If your synth is capable of cross-modulation, tune two oscillators an octave apart. Raise the filter frequency and turn on the signal from the oscillator to be modulated (the modulation destination). Route any waveform from the modulating oscillator (the source) to modify the frequency of the other oscillator (the destination). Play the keyboard. Now gradually lower the frequency of the higher oscillator. Stop and play awhile whenever the resulting timbre grabs your ear.

PATCH PROGRAMMING

Most synthesizers can produce an almost incredible variety of sounds, sounds which may be programmed by anyone with the necessary skills. Programming synth sounds isn't difficult if you understand the basics, nor is it something you can completely master in half an hour. The parameters of each sound are collected into patch programs, which are stored in the synthesizer's built-in digital memory to be recalled at the touch of a button. A synth may sound like a 20-foot trumpet, or rubber violins, or an underwater buzzsaw, depending on which program is called up.

Programming a synthesizer is not the same as programming a computer. You don't have to learn any specialized languages, but you must have a working knowledge of synthesis. Without learning to program, you just can't get the most out of your synthesizer. By adjusting individual parameters, you define the details of any sound your synth makes. Parameters are changed by altering the synthesizer's front panel control settings. Once you get a patch just the way you want it, just press a couple of switches and it's stored permanently. By assigning a program number to that sound, you can retrieve it at any time. Several synths even remember patch names. A recalled patch can be edited, and the changes can be memorized as part of that patch or stored as a whole new patch.

Analog synthesizers have parameter settings which are continuously variable, that is, they can be changed by any degree of different values within their specified ranges. To control these values with a microprocessor, however, they must be specified as numbers, which means each range must be quantized into discrete steps. A synth might offer 16 modulation depth settings, for example, but 128 different settings for filter frequency. Obviously, the greater number of quantized values gives you increased parameter control. When a parameter is specified as one of two possible states, like on and off, a switch does the job.

DATA ENTRY SYSTEMS

Every synthesizer has a limited number of user-programmable parameters. Some instruments give you access to virtually every parameter imaginable, but others restrict access to as few as 20 specific parameters. The front panels of older, analog synthesizers are filled with pots and switches, each one controlling just one or two parameters. A separate control for each function makes it easy to look at the panel and figure out how a sound is programmed. When programmable patch memory came along in 1978, synthesists gained the ability to quickly call up programs, but lost the ability to see every parameter setting at a glance. It's impossible for every knob and switch to physically change its position whenever the program number is changed.

Many instruments still have separate controls for each parameter, but many more have fewer controls which serve multiple functions. Some, like the Roland Super Jupiter and JX-8P, have full panel programmers available as optional accessories. A number of synthesizers, from the Sequential SixTrak to the Synclavier, have only one knob or slider which controls every user-programmable parameter, one or more switches to choose which parameter it's controlling, and numeric or alphanumeric displays to indicate the parameter and its value. Other control panels have buttons which let you specify a 2-digit number for the parameter and another 2-digit number for its value. Many more have only two switches for incremental control: one for increasing a parameter's value and another for decreasing it. The obvious advantage is that less hardware saves money, but only at the expense of easy programmability. The best way to deal with a single-parameter-at-a-time data entry system is to use a personal computer with voice editor software, which makes it easy to visualize how each setting contributes to the overall sound. Other instruments, like the Oberheim Matrix-12 and Chroma Polaris, compromise with assignable pots and switches controlling several parameters each.

PATCH EDITING

When a program is recalled from memory, parameter data is transferred to a memory buffer. The buffer then contains a temporary copy of the program, recorded from permanent memory. Because the front panel controls only change what's stored in the buffer, you can edit these parameters without affecting what's stored in the memory banks. Most synthesizers with a number of parameter controls have pots and switches which are activated whenever their values are changed. As soon as a knob detects that it's being turned, or a switch is pressed, it accepts its new value and changes the patch accordingly. A few instruments have pots which change parameter values by whatever degree their positions are changed, rather than jumping to the value indicated by their positions. Editing programs lets you improve stored patches, or construct new sounds from similar ones.

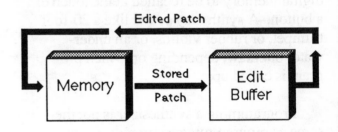

Once a program has been edited, it may be stored in the synthesizer's permanent memory. Many instruments feature a "write protect" switch, usually on the back panel, which must be disabled to store any new programs. (Consult your owner's manual for details.) When you assign a program number to your new patch, you're erasing whatever program previously filled that memory slot. Most synthesizers provide some method of comparing an edited patch with the permanently stored version, so you can switch between the two. It's a good idea to leave certain program slots empty for storing new patches until they find a permanent home. If your synth doesn't display the name of each program, it's important that you keep a list of stored patch programs so you don't erase one you really want to keep.

PATCH MEMORY

User-programmable synthesizers have what's called non-volatile memory, which means that the data is preserved even when the instrument is turned off. Non-volatile memory is powered by a long-life battery inside the synth. These batteries normally last for five to ten years, at which time they must be recharged or replaced, usually by a service technician. Fortunately, it's possible to off-load patch programs to other forms of memory storage.

The most popular media of external data storage include cassette, RAM cartridge, and computer disk. Most synthesizers feature a cassette interface, input and output jacks for dumping and loading program data to and from standard audio tapes. You can often transfer individual programs or entire sets to tape for permanent storage. New synthesizers are often shipped with cassettes containing all the factory-programmed patches, and you can buy or trade cassettes with new sounds programmed for your particular synth. Cassette recorders have different input and output levels, so you may have to experiment before you find the best machine or the correct record and playback settings for your synth. When data is dumped to tape, you can usually run a verify procedure to insure that the data is properly recorded. You may load an entire set of programs from cassette into the instrument's permanent memory, or load just one program to the temporary buffer.

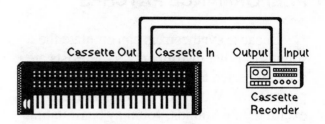

Some synthesizers store programs on RAM cartridges, which are really electrically erasable ROM cartridges. The chief advantage is almost instantaneous program loading, but RAM cartridges cost a great deal more than cassettes. A handful of instruments have built-in floppy disk drives, which give you the dual advantage of instant loading and an inexpensive storage medium. A typical floppy disk costs less than a good quality cassette, but the drives add to the expense of the instrument. Now you can get floppy disk drives which attach to the MIDI output of your synth to record patches.

If you have a personal computer, the best way to store patch programs is with patch librarian software, which lets you store data on computer disk via the MIDI interface. The best patch librarians let you rearrange patches and reassign program names and numbers. Unless you have one of the more popular models, it may be difficult to find a patch librarian for your synthesizer which is compatible with your particular computer. Someday soon, though, you should be able to dump program data from almost any MIDI synth directly onto computer disk.

PERFORMANCE PATCHES

Because synthesizers can emulate the sounds of other instruments, synthesists are often expected to substitute for other performers. When you're not inventing exciting, new sounds, you may be imitating traditional tone colors. Even if you don't like the idea of trying to sound like something acoustic, mimicking other instruments is an excellent way to learn the basics of synthesizer programming.

First, understand that it's very difficult to precisely duplicate any acoustical sound with analog electronics. Even if you have a digital synth, you can't fool all of the people all of the time. Analog synth oscillators generate very pure waveforms with mathematically perfect harmonic structures. Real-life acoustical mathematics is seldom so perfect. Most acoustic instruments produce slightly out-of-tune harmonics with very complex phase relationships. If your instrument is capable of reproducing that kind of complexity, you can synthesize very realistic instrumental timbres. With analog oscillators and filters, you can still come close enough to convince most listeners.

The biggest stumbling block which the synthesist faces in replicating other instruments is learning to play idiomatically. An oboe player, for instance, spends his entire musical education learning to play within the limitations of the oboe. If you want to synthesize an oboe, you have to play within those same limitations. A keyboard instrument, unlike most others, has semitones lined up adjacent to one another. A guitarist never plays block chords exactly the way an pianist does. Phrasing and articulation are critical.

With the limitations of analog synthesis in mind, let's examine a few sounds and how you might go about synthesizing them. For the purposes of this discussion, let's assume that your synth has what's become the standard synthesizer voice: two oscillators, a lowpass filter, an amplifier, an LFO, and two ADSR generators. If not, compensate. Because every synthesizer is different, precise parameter settings are impossible to prescribe. Instead, we can only suggest general guidelines to steer you in the right direction. Your ears have to take it from there.

Hammond Organ: The sound of the Hammond organ has almost always been popular in rock music. The Hammond B-3 is a type of additive synthesizer dating back to the 1930s. Each drawbar controls the amplitude of one harmonic tone. Drawbar combinations yield different harmonic spectra, giving the organist a variety of complex waveforms. Because the key contacts don't always hit all the harmonic busses at the same instant, the keyboard can be slightly touch-sensitive. The vibrato is mechanical rather than electronic, so it actually modulates the waveform a bit. All these factors produce an almost acoustic-sounding timbre you can listen to for long periods of time without aural fatigue. The standard practice of playing through a rotating loudspeaker adds even more motion to the Hammond sound.

To approximate a Hammond timbre, tune oscillator 1 to its middle range. Tune the second oscillator a perfect 12th (an octave + a 5th) higher than the first and then sync them. (Most synthesizers sync oscillator 2 to oscillator 1. If your synth has it backwards, reverse this procedure.) Both waveforms are square, but try other pulse widths for a wider range of tone colors. Turn the filter up over halfway and let the keyboard modulate its frequency. A little resonance brightens the color, if you like. If you want a percussive effect, the filter envelope settings should all be at zero, with perhaps the initial decay just barely above zero. The envelope depth controls the amount of key click. If you don't want percussion, don't modulate the filter with an envelope at all. The amplifier envelope is typically organ-like: instant attack, full sustain, and instant release. For a punchier sound, cut the sustain to about half, with a short initial decay. For vibrato, modulate the pulse width of both oscillators with the LFO. If you can control PWM depth with the modulation controller, so much the better. If you have outboard signal processors, chorus and reverb make a nice combination.

Combo Organ: Tune two oscillators a perfect 12th apart and sync them. (For playing in the lower registers, try an interval of a perfect 5th.) Use narrow pulse waves, or perhaps a sawtooth from either oscillator. Turn the filter frequency up all the way, with resonance to taste. The amplifier envelope has instant attack, full sustain, and instant release. Vibrato is an essential ingredient in the combo organ sound, about 10 Hz at a moderate depth.

Pipe Organ: A convincing pipe organ requires more than two oscillators. If you can layer voices, tune at least four oscillators in successive octaves: 32', 16', 8', and 4'. (Incidentally, references to footage are derived from the actual lengths of organ pipes.) Waveforms are square, and the sync

is switched off. Filter frequency is up full, unless a mellower sound is desired, and the resonance is turned down. Attack is not quite zero, full sustain, and a short release. Reverb helps to give the illusion of a large hall, the natural habitat of pipe organs.

Clavinet: The Clavinet is an electro-acoustic approximation of the clavichord, an instrument which predates both the harpsichord and piano. Synthesizers take the approximation a logical step further. Tune both oscillators to their medium low range, narrow pulse width, in unison. Turn the filter frequency down and the envelope depth up. Let it track the keyboard slightly. Resonance is optional. Filter attack, sustain, and release are all minimum, with initial decay just over a second, depending on your phrasing. Amplifier envelope is instant on, medium decay, no sustain, and instant off. Modulate the pulse width just a little with the filter's envelope generator. Clavinet play-ing is characterized by sparse, choppy licks and octave bass lines.

Piano: Acoustic piano is one of the most difficult instruments to realistically synthesize, because its waveform is so dynamically complex. Each note has one, two, or three strings, depending on its pitch. Harmonic relationships are constantly changing. The overtones aren't precise multiples of the fundamental frequency. As the harmonic number increases, the frequency of each partial is a few cents sharper in relation to the fundamental. The 2nd, 3rd, and 4th harmonics are stronger than the fundamental, each with its own envelope. Sound energy constantly shifts from one harmonic to another, but the total sound dies away evenly.

If you have a sufficiently complex digital synthesizer, perhaps you can tune and shape each overtone. Otherwise, tune oscillator 1 to its middle range, and tune oscillator 2 a major 20th (two octaves + a M6th) higher. Pulse width for both oscillators is around 25%. The initial filter cutoff frequency is about half, with the envelope depth also about half, and with plenty of keyboard tracking. The filter envelope has instant attack, with medium decay, sustain, and release. For the amplifier envelope, try instant attack, medium decay or longer, sustain under half, with a fairly short release. Adjust your settings to suit what you're playing. If you can extend release time with a footpedal, it makes a fine sustain pedal for piano sounds.

Bass: Obviously, the formula for programming bass depends on the type of bass sound you want. The role of bass has been played by many instruments, including synthesizer. There are fat-sounding basses, thin-sounding basses, electric basses, acoustic basses, slapped basses, fretless basses — you get the idea. Well, here's a place to start, then it's up to you.

Begin with two oscillators in their lowest audio range, either in unison or tuned an octave apart, with the sync on or off. Waveform is sawtooth, and if available, a triangle wave to emphasize the fundamental. Turn the filter frequency down and the filter envelope amount up at least halfway, or to the desired level of brightness. Resonance depends on how much of a wah effect you want. Set the filter attack at zero, medium short decay, sustain under half, and a short release. For the amplifier envelope, instant attack, medium short decay, and zero

sustain. Release time is generally rather short, but can be adjusted to suit your phrasing. Try layering as many bass voices as you can for a fat synth-bass sound. Feel free to bend notes and add vibrato as you play.

Brass: Brass instruments and synthesized brass are often used to spice up rock arrangements. These include trumpet, trombone, French horn, tuba, and brass ensemble. Most of the time, the trumpet's tone is particularly bright and clear. Sawtooth is the only appropriate waveform for all brass instruments. Tune both oscillators to the middle register. Sync them for solo trumpet, no sync for ensemble. For ensemble, detune them slightly. Turn down the filter frequency and the resonance. Filter envelope amount is up most of the way, depending on the desired degree of brilliance. Add enough keyboard tracking to brighten up the top. Delayed filter vibrato works well.

The envelopes are a bit tricky, and the exact settings differ for almost every synthesizer. The amplifier has a fast but not instant attack, with a medium fast decay, three-quarter sustain, and a short release. The filter envelope is adjusted relative to the amplifier envelope. Filter attack is between two and three times as long as amplifier attack. You must rely on your ears to find just the right combination of attack characteristics which sound most trumpet-like. The most minute changes in filter attack make a noticeable difference. The initial decay is also crucial. It's brief, but longer than the amplifier decay, and the sustain is barely over halfway up. Release is slightly longer than the amplifier release. Take the time to discover the best envelope settings for your instrument.

Other brass sounds are variations on the trumpet. French horn has a slightly longer attack (most of the time). There's less keyboard and envelope modulation of the filter, dulling the tone somewhat. Flugelhorn sounds a lot like trumpet, though also not as bright. Trombone is an octave lower, with a longer filter attack. It helps a lot if you can modulate the filter with the LFO, with about a one-second delay. Trombones can slide, so apply portamento and slow vibrato, but don't overdo it. For tuba, switch the oscillators to their lowest audio range and the sustain to just under half. A tuba's attack is slower than other brass, and the filter opens only about halfway.

Strings: The sound of an orchestral string ensemble is one of the most frequently synthesized. The combination of violin, viola, cello, and/or bowed bass blends well with almost any instrumental palette. You may try to duplicate real strings as closely as possible, or you may just want an impression of strings to fulfill the same role of harmonic accompaniment.

First, let's examine the properties of the violin sound. When a violin is bowed, friction sets the string in motion as the resin-coated bow tugs at the string and then releases it suddenly, hundreds or thousands of times a second. The string vibrates the bridge, which vibrates the violin body, which in turn vibrates the surrounding air. Parts of the instrument resonate at different frequencies. In a good violin, the resonances are evenly distributed throughout its range. That way, its total acoustical output is maximized, and there's little variation in output anywhere on the fingerboard.

As the violin is played, the waveform changes dynamically. Every note has its own spectrum. The amplitudes and phase relationships of the harmonics are in constant flux. When vibrato is employed, some partials are shifted out of tune with others. Synthesizing a realistic solo violin with analog electronics is not an easy task, but synthesizing an ensemble isn't difficult.

Tune your oscillators in unison, but detune them slightly so they drift in and out of phase. Range depends on which stringed instruments you want to synthesize. As for waveform, start with 30% pulse waves. Modulate the pulse width with a 5-7 Hz sine or triangle wave at a moderate depth. It's important to hear harmonic motion within the waveform, so a pulse waveform is the only logical choice. Most synthesizers have no means for changing the shape of sawtooth waves with an LFO. If you prefer the sound of a sawtooth, try mixing sawtooth and modulated pulse.

Adjust the filter frequency up about one-third, with no resonance. Filter envelope amount is nearly full for violins, less for other strings. You may weaken the first harmonic with a highpass filter if you want a thinner tone. The envelope times depend on the rhythm of what you're playing. Faster passages demand less time than slower ones. Start with a medium filter attack, medium short decay, sustain about three-quarters, with a medium short release. As a general rule, make the attack time a bit longer than the release. For shaping the loudness contour, attack and release are just a touch faster than the filter attack and release, with full sustain.

String technique is very dependent on vibrato. Each player in an ensemble applies a different rate and depth of vibrato. If you can, use separate LFOs to modulate each oscillator. If that's not possible, perhaps you can at least modulate them at different depths. The vibrato depth is slightly greater than for most instrumental vibratos, but the rate is about the same. Because a synth sounds less like real strings without vibrato, delayed vibrato isn't very effective. To make your string sound really authentic, manually alter both the depth and rate of vibrato during a sustained note or chord. If possible, the vibrato source should be different from the source of pulse width modulation.

Playing idiomatically is very important. Many keyboardists play polyphonic strings in block chords, like they play organ. Real strings are seldom orchestrated in such close harmony, particularly in the lower registers. Allow larger intervals, and remember the magic word: simplify. There's no need to play every possible note in a chord. Listen to real string ensembles, both modern and classical, to develop a feel for their phrasing.

Outboard effects can be quite useful in your quest for the perfect string timbre. Reverb is a great help, especially for creating the impression of a large ensemble. An equalizer (preferably parametric) is indispensable for duplicating the many resonances in an ensemble of strings. Chorusing can fatten up the sound and provide another source of harmonic motion. Don't forget, even if what you find doesn't sound exactly like real violins and cellos, it may be just as useful.

Buyer's Guide to Synthesizers

Which synthesizer is the right one for you? Is one instrument enough? Are six too many? The tremendous variety of synthesizers on the market today can make those decisions a difficult task. If you spend all your money on an instrument that doesn't do what you need, or one that's uncomfortable to play or too complicated to ever understand, it can be an expensive mistake. Despite falling prices, synthesizers aren't cheap. Armed with a little knowledge, though, you can probably find the one model that best suits your needs and desires.

When shopping for a synth, take the time to compare features and functions. Don't get stuck with something you'll outgrow in a month's time. When you buy a brand new synthesizer, its resale value almost always depreciates immediately. If you're unhappy with your purchase and you want to dump it, don't expect to get back what you paid. Still, keep in mind that it's unlikely that any synth will fulfill all your synthesizing needs forever. Musical technology is advancing at a rapid pace, and it probably will for some time to come. New instruments are constantly introduced that make older models seem outmoded and obsolete.

When you decide to part with your money, your choices are many. Be sure to check out various makes and models before arriving at a final decision. Shop around — the price of a particular model may vary drastically from store to store. Ask lots of questions. Can it be serviced locally? Does it come with a warranty? Why is the salesman trying to get me to buy that synth instead of the one I came in here to buy?

The bottom line when searching for any instrument is, does it sound good? In a store, listen to the instruments you're considering with reverb and other external effects all turned off. If your compare the sound of two different synthesizers, you're likely to notice tonal differences. The most obvious reason is because of different filter designs. One filter may have a relatively flat frequency bandwidth, where another may boost the bass or midrange frequencies. Filters also have different cutoff slopes. Digital envelope generators are faster than analog envelope generators. Two-stage envelope generators can't sound like 8-stage envelope generators. Software-generated oscillators don't sound like analog VCOs.

See and play a number of instruments before you make your final decision. No two synthesizer models are alike. You must consider your intended applications, as well as your budget, when making a choice. How much can you afford? Why do you want a synthesizer? Do you need a digital synth or an analog/digital hybrid? How many voices? Should it have a keyboard, or do you have enough keyboards already? Do you need a touch-sensitive key-board? Weighted action? Split keyboard? Should it have a built-in sequencer? What kind of sequencer? Do you plan to control your synth with a personal computer? What kind of computer? Are you going to do your own patch programming? Do you have a preference for off-line data storage? What about sampling keyboards? How about a used instrument? Do you really need MIDI? What are you going to interface it to? Should you buy now or wait for the next big thing? What are your choices?

KEYBOARD SYNTHESIZERS

The **Yamaha DX7** is the flagship of their DX series of all-digital FM synthesizers. The first of a new generation of user-programmable digital instruments, the DX7 is extremely popular on stage and in the studio. It features 16 voices with six operators and 32 algorithms per voice, a keyboard which is both velocity- and pressure-sensitive, and an optional breath controller. Each operator has an 8-stage envelope generator, and 32 programs are stored internally. ROM and RAM cartridges expand program memory by 64 and 32 programs, respectively.

The top-of-the-line **Yamaha DX1** has twice the sound-generating capability of the DX7 for layered sounds and splits. It offers 32 voices, multiple parameter displays, 64-program internal memory, and two cartridge slots for up to 128-program ROM cartridge storage. The **DX5** is very similar to the DX1, but with fewer displays, fewer controls, and a lower price.

The **Yamaha DX9** is a scaled-down DX7 with only four operators and eight algorithms per voice, only 20 internal voice programs, no touch sensitivity, and no cartridge storage. Yamaha's **DX21**, an 8-voice instrument, also with four operators and eight algorithms, stores and recalls 32 patches, which may be user-programmed or loaded from 128 internal presets. The keyboard can be split and patches can be layered, with separate outputs for each half. Another 4-operator synthesizer, the **DX-27**

has 192 presets stored in ROM, with 24 user-programmable patches, plus a velocity-sensitive keyboard and a chorus effect. It's available with a pair of amplified speakers as the **DX27S**. The **DX-100** is identical to the DX27, except for a smaller keyboard.

From Fender, the **Chroma Polaris** is a mostly digital, 6-voice synthesizer with an analog filter and two analog oscillators per voice, 132 patch programs, a velocity-sensitive keyboard, the ability to split and layer programs, both pulse and sawtooth waveform modulation, ring modulation, extensive sync capabilities, and a real-time sequencer which memorizes all parameter and patch changes and responds to the tempo with which you tap a footswitch. Under MIDI control, the Polaris becomes fully multi-timbral, able to produce any six of eight different sounds simultaneously.

A refugee from ARP Instruments, the **Rhodes Chroma** stores 50 patches and has 16 channels, each with an oscillator, filter, and amplifier. Normally, channels are paired for 8-voice polyphony, but 16 distinct configurations are possible, including the ability to layer eight sounds per key. A master control slider and flat membrane switches select modes and functions, retrieve patches, and give you access to virtually every conceivable parameter. The wooden, weighted, velocity-sensitive keyboard offers pressure-sensitivity as an option. Both Chromas feature the 25-pin Chroma computer interface.

Roland makes the **Jupiter-8**, an 8-voice synth with 64-program memory, split keyboard and patch layering, sample & hold, an arpeggiator, and extensive left-hand modulation controls. The Jupiter-8 has a manual highpass filter, and the lowpass filter has selectable rolloff. The 6-voice **Jupiter-6** features two LFOs, arpeggio, both portamento and glissando, 2-way oscillator sync, and invertible envelopes. Oscillator cross-modulation depth can be controlled by an envelope, and the multimode filter has inputs from either ADSR generator.

Another Roland, the **Juno-106**, is a 6-voice synth with one DCO plus a sub-octave generator per voice, a noise generator, a single invertable ADSR generator, front panel MIDI switching, polyphonic portamento, and stereo chorusing. The Juno-106 stores 128 patches and has stereo outputs. The **Roland Synth Plus-60** is similar to the Juno-106, with a pair of built-in speakers. Each voice of Roland's **Juno 1** features one oscillator with 14 waveforms and an 8-stage envelope generator. It has a 4-octave keyboard and memorizes 64 patches. The **Juno 2** adds a RAM cartridge slot, plus a 5-octave, velocity- and pressure-sensitive keyboard.

Roland's **JX-8P**, yet another 6-voice, has two DCOs and two ADSR generators per voice. The keyboard is both velocity- and pressure-sensitive, and you can assign one, two, or six voices to each key. The alpha-numeric display lets you name patches, and a single slider is used to alter parameters. The optional PG800 programmer module gives you access to all programmable parameters. The expandable memory has 64 factory presets and 32 user-programmable patches.

The 12-voice **Roland JX-10**, also called the Super JX, has 50 user-programmable patches and a cartridge slot for 50 more, 50 presets, a sequencer, and a velocity- and pressure-sensitive keyboard with programmable splits and layering.

Oberheim's **Matrix-12** is a 12-voice, fully multi-timbral synthesizer with 100 patch programs and another 100 programs which store multi-patches, containing multiple splits, layering, MIDI channel and keyboard assignments, plus the relative balance, detuning, and stereo panning of the voices. The keyboard can be split into six zones, each with an assigned patch, or you can assign up to six voices to each key. The individual voices, parameter control, and modulation routing are almost identical to the Oberheim Xpander (see page 99). Their 6-voice **Matrix-6** stores 100 patch programs and 50 multi-patch programs. It features a velocity- and pressure-sensitive keyboard, splits and layering, with two DCOs, three DADSR generators, and one 4-pole filter per voice.

Korg makes the **Poly-800II**, with a pair of DCOs and three 6-stage envelope generators per voice, and 64-patch memory. The eight voices share a single parapolyphonic filter, and a polyphonic, step time sequencer stores 1000 notes. Programmable digital delay and equalization are built in. The lightweight Poly-800II is powered by batteries or an AC adapter.

The 8-voice **Korg DW-8000** stores 64 programs, and it has a lowpass filter, two 6-stage envelopes, and two oscillators per voice with 16 complex digital waveforms each. The weighted keyboard is both velocity- and pressure-sensitive, and like the Poly-800II, its left-hand controller is a joystick. Other features include a programmable digital delay and an arpeggiator. The **DW-6000** has six voices, two oscillators with eight waveforms per voice, a chorus circuit instead of digital delay, and no touch-sensitivity.

The latest incarnation of Sequential's ground-breaking Prophet synthesizer is the **Prophet VS**, an 8-voice instrument with four digital oscillators per voice. Each oscillator can produce 128 waveforms, including 32 user-definable waveforms. Using a technique called vector synthesis, the combination of the four waveforms is controlled by a joystick, an envelope generator, or keyboard velocity. Other features include a velocity-sensitive keyboard with aftertouch, splits and layering, 5-stage envelope generators, analog filters, two arpeggiators, programmable stereo panning and chorusing, and the ability to store and recall up to 200 patch programs via RAM and ROM cartridges.

The 6-voice **Siel DK 700** synthesizer stores 73 programs and 55 program/channel combinations. Each voice contains two DCOs, a VCF, and a single ADSR. There are three LFOs and a velocity-sensitive keyboard. The velocity-sensitive **Siel DK 80** is a 12-voice synth with stereo layering and a 2-track sequencer. It holds 40 presets and 10 user-programmable sounds, plus up to 100 more on cartridge. Each voice contains a DCO, a VCF, two envelope generators, and two LFOs. The **DK 70** memorizes the same number of patches and presets, but in an 8-voice configuration with a strap-on option.

The Casio CZ series, beginning with the ever-popular **CZ101**, use a unique digital technique called phase distortion synthesis. It has a mini-keyboard, 16 factory presets, and 16 user-programmable voices. Each voice has a single software-generated oscillator and three 8-stage envelope generators. The CZ101 has up to eight voices, but they can be combined into four 2-oscillator voices or two 4-oscillator voices. Under MIDI control, the CZ101 becomes a 4-voice multi-timbral slave instrument. The **Casio CZ1000** is almost identical, but with a full-size keyboard.

Casio's **CZ-1** is an 8-voice, multi-timbral instrument with 64 presets, 64 user programs, and a cartridge input for another 64 sounds. The CZ-1 has portamento and chorusing, and its split keyboard is both pressure- and velocity-sensitive. The **CZ5000** features 16 single oscillator voices, eight 2-oscillator voices, or four 4-oscillator voices, and can produce eight different sounds under MIDI control. It stores 32 presets and 32 user programs, and it has many performance controls. The keyboard isn't touch-sensitive, but the on-board, 8-track, multi-timbral sequencer stores 3500 notes in real time or 7000 notes in step time. The similar **CZ-3000** has no sequencer.

The 6-voice **Akai AX60** holds 64 patches and eight keyboard split presets. Each voice has one VCO, one ADSR generator, and analog filtering. Other features include a noise generator, chorusing, unison mode, and an arpeggiator. The **AX73** is another 6-voice unit, but with a 73-key, velocity-sensitive keyboard, stereo chorus, and two ADSRs per voice. The AX73 stores 100 patch programs.

The **Ensoniq ESQ-1** is an 8-voice, multi-timbral synthesizer with three oscillators per voice, each with 32 sampled and synthesized digital waveforms, and a weighted, velocity-sensitive keyboard. It stores 40 patches, with another 80 available on cartridge. The ESQ-1 features extensive modulation capabilities, including four envelope generators per voice, programmable panning, chorus, and ring modulation. Its 8-track sequencer can record up to eight voices per track, with up to 30 sequences chained to form 10 songs. Sequencer memory is expandable from 2400 to 10,000 notes. The sequencer also features selectable autocorrection and sync-to-tape.

The **Kawai 240** is an 8-voice synth with 48 patch programs, a 1500-note, real time sequencer, splits and doubles, ring modulation, and an alphanumeric display for naming programs and sequences. There are two DCOs per voice, but the second one is strictly square wave. Kawai's **K-3** synthesizer features additive waveform synthesis and analog filtering, with a weighted, pressure-sensitive keyboard.

The **PPG Wave 2.3**, from Germany, is an update of the Wave 2.2. It has eight multi-timbral voices, each with two digital wavetable oscillators, two ADSRs, an AD generator, and an analog filter. The Wave's memory stores 87 programs plus 20 sets of eight program assignments called combiprograms. The velocity- and pressure-sensitive keyboard splits into eight zones, and the sequencer records eight tracks. With the addition of the **PPG Waveterm B** computer, you can sample sounds and create your own voices by additive synthesis. An **Expansion Voice Unit** (EVU) adds another eight voices to the PPG system. The optional **PRK FD** is a 6-octave, wooden, weighted keyboard with an integrated 99-track sequencer and a 5-1/4" disk drive.

MIDI MODULAR SYSTEMS

One of the most flexible MIDI synth expanders made is the **Oberheim Xpander**. It's a 6-voice, multi-timbral instrument with audio outputs for each voice and inputs for MIDI controllers and for control voltages and gates from non-MIDI controllers. The Xpander stores 100 patch programs, and there's a 120-character alphanumeric display window for naming patches and keeping track of functions. Each voice has two analog oscillators, fifteen amplifiers, a 15-mode filter, five DADSR generators, five LFOs, and numerous other signal processors. The Xpander responds to velocity- and pressure-sensitive keyboards, and there are 47 modulation destinations with 27 sources per voice, making it the modern, digitally-controlled equivalent of an old-fashioned, modular, patchcord synth. For a lot less money, the **Oberheim Matrix-6R** is a keyboardless, rack-mountable version of their Matrix-6.

Also from Oberheim, the **Xk** keyboard features velocity- and pressure-sensitivity. The 5-octave keyboard can be split into three zones, each sending on a different MIDI channel, and an arpeggiator can be assigned to one channel. The Xk's 100 programs recall patch numbers, zone locations, and other parameters.

The rack-mountable **Roland MKS-80 Super Jupiter** has the best features of both the Jupiter-6 and the Jupiter-8, in an 8-voice configuration with a new filter and no keyboard. The Super Jupiter's programmable memory contains 64 patches plus 64 pairs of patches. The liquid crystal display shows not only numbers and letters, but symbols representing waveforms. Sounds can be split and layered, and parameter changes are made with four buttons. If you prefer a full control panel with knobs and sliders, the Super Jupiter Programmer is available as an option. The **MKS-70 Super JX** is another rack module with 12 voices, 50 presets, and 50 programmable patches. The **MKS-30 Planet-S** is a six-voice expander module which stores 64 programs in memory and another 64 in cartridge.

Roland makes a variety of MIDI keyboards to suit your needs and your budget. The **MKB-1000** 88-note keyboard has a weighted, wooden action and adjustable velocity-sensitivity. The programmable, floating split can be assigned to any two MIDI channels. The 128-program memory stores sets of information on modes, channels, and split points, as well as program numbers. The 76-key **MKB-300** has the same features with a more conventional plastic keyboard. Another MIDI keyboard, the **MKB-200**, is both velocity- and pressure-sensitive. The **Roland Axis** is a strap-on, velocity- and pressure-sensitive keyboard with 128 patch locations and remote autotune. Other features include programmable switches, wheel controllers, and a foot pedal.

The **Octave-plateau Voyetra Eight** is an rack-mountable, 8-voice synth module with extensive modulation routing. It stores 100 patch programs and another 100 programs specifying keyboard splits and layering, balance levels, arpeggiator settings, and other parameter assignments. The Voyetra's real time sequencer stores about 850 notes, and sequences can be overdubbed. In addition to XLR MIDI jacks, there are back panel control voltage and gate jacks for controlling a monophonic, non-MIDI synthesizer. The optional **VPK-5** keyboard is both velocity- and pressure-sensitive, and pitch bend and modulation are controlled with a joystick.

Yamaha's **TX816** FM Tone Generator System is the keyboardless equivalent of eight DX7s, each with 16 voices, in a rack-mountable unit. Each voice module is a **TF1**, and each TF1 can store 32 programs, including voice and function parameters. By defining the upper and lower note limits of each channel, the TX816 lets you assign each module to a specific keyboard zone, permitting multiple splits and layering. The TF1 has no patch editing facilities, but voices may be loaded and edited from a DX1, DX5, or a DX7, or with DX-voicing software for a personal computer. The **Yamaha TX216** is basically the same unit, but with only two TF1s.

The **TX7** is a budget-minded version of the 6-operator FM Tone Generator, also with 32 patch programs, plus 32 function programs for a DX7 or a DX9. Function parameters may be edited from the panel, but like the TX816, voice parameter editing requires that you use a DX keyboard synth or editing software. Programs can be stored on cassette, and programs can be transferred from a DX synthesizer. Yamaha's **FB-01** Tone Generator is a stereo, multi-timbral module with eight 4-operator voices and 16 user-programmable configurations. It contains 240 presets in ROM and stores 96 programmable patches.

Yamaha's 88-key, weighted, MIDI keyboard controller, the **KX88**, responds to velocity and pressure, and features programmable Moog-style wheels, sliders, and switches for controlling MIDI functions and parameter assignments. There are 16 programs for storing controller assignments, keyboard splits, and MIDI information. The **KX1** and **KX5** are Yamaha's more portable, strap-on keyboards.

Akai makes a 6-voice rack-mount synthesizer called the **VX90**. It has most features of their AX73, with no keyboard and no chorusing. Akai also makes the velocity-sensitive **MX73** keyboard with 100 patch positions, programmable sliders and switches, and a liquid crystal display.

The **Casio AZ-1** is an 8-voice, strap-on, velocity- and pressure-sensitive keyboard with assignable thumbwheels, switches, and a slider. It can send 128 patch changes on two MIDI channels at once.

The **Korg EX-800** is basically a keyboardless Poly-800, with a few more user controls and the ability to layer sounds. The **EX-8000** is a modular version of the Korg DW-8000. Their **RK-100** is a strap-on MIDI keyboard with 64 program locations, octave switching, and wheels for controlling volume, pitch bend, and assignable modulation.

SAMPLING INSTRUMENTS

Sequential's **Prophet 2000** is an 8-voice instrument with the ability to sample sounds up to 16 seconds long, with an 7.8 kHz bandwidth. There are three selectable sampling rates, with a maximum bandwidth of 20 kHz for a 6-second sample. Up to 16 samples may be layered or assigned across the keyboard. A built-in microfloppy disk drive lets you store and retrieve samples and processing parameters. Twelve preset waveforms are stored in memory, and all sounds may be processed by a lowpass filter, an amplifier, two ADSR envelopes, and a built-in delay line. The Prophet 2000 features a weighted, velocity-sensitive keyboard and an arpeggiator. The **Prophet 2002** is a rack-mounted, keyboardless version of the 2000.

E-mu's **Emulator II** records 17.6-second samples with a full 20 kHz bandwidth for a single sample. Different samples may be assigned to each key, but you can only play eight voices at once. Each voice has a lowpass filter, amplifier, LFO, and two ADSR generators. The weighted keyboard is velocity-sensitive, and either left-hand wheel may be programmed to control pitch bend, filter cutoff, attack rate, and LFO modulation of frequency, filter, or amplifier. Sounds can be looped, truncated, transposed, and spliced together. The Emulator II includes an 8-track MIDI sequencer with editing and autocorrection, one or two 5-1/4" disk drives, a SMPTE generator and reader, and an RS-422 port. The **Emulator II+** has twice the sampling time of the Emulator II.

The **E-mu Emax** has eight sampling rates, with 17 seconds sampling time at 28 kHz. It's an 8-voice instrument with two samples per voice, eight outputs, and up to 122 samples across the keyboard. The Emax features analog processing, a multitrack sequencer, and both velocity- and pressure-sensitivity. A rack-mount, modular version is also available.

When the **Kurzweil 250** was introduced, it gained worldwide attention with its ability to reproduce the nuances of a grand piano. With an 88-key, velocity-sensitive, weighted, wooden keyboard, the K250 has 12 voices and 30 factory-sampled sounds, with additional sounds available. The 12-channel sequencer holds up to 7500 notes, but can be expanded to hold over 15,000. Sounds can be processed by a 256-stage envelope, chorusing, tremolo, doubling, flanging, echo, portamento, etc. User sampling is available as an option, as is the ability to resynthesize sounds and transcribe musical scores.

The **Kurzweil 150 Expander** is a module which divides a keyboard into three zones, each zone containing up to seven layers. It responds to polyphonic key pressure and velocity. The K150 Expander is a preset instrument, but additional sound blocks may be added.

The **Ensoniq Mirage** is widely regarded as the poor man's Emulator. Up to 16 samples can be spread across its velocity-sensitive keyboard. Samples are stored on microfloppies with the built-in disk drive. The maximum sampling rate is 33 kHz for 2.2 seconds, with a minimum 4 kHz rate for 8.8 seconds. A real time sequencer is expandable by means of a RAM cartridge. User sampling is simplified with optional computer software. The **Mirage Digital Multi-Sampler** is a rack-mount Mirage without the keyboard.

Another rack-mount sampler, the **Akai S-612,** is a 6-voice module with a maximum sampling rate of 32 kHz and a maximum sampling time of eight seconds. Samples can be edited, overdubbed, and spliced. The S-612 can transmit and receive on MIDI channels 1-9. Sounds are stored on 2.8-inch disks using the optional MD-280 drive. Akai's more powerful **S-900** sampler features eight polytimbral voices with eight individual outputs, 32 sample points, and a 40 kHz sampling rate. Each voice has an ADSR generator, an LFO, and an analog filter.

The **Roland S-50** is a 16-voice, velocity- and pressure-sensitive keyboard sampler with two 8-stage envelope generators, an analog filter, and one LFO per voice. Total sampling time is 15 or 30 seconds at a rate of either 30 or 15 kHz. Up to 16 samples may be spread across the keys. The built-in disk drive stores samples on 3.5-inch disks. All parameters may be viewed and edited by connecting a monitor and a computer keyboard to the S-50. The **S-10** is an 8-voice sampler with a smaller, velocity-sensitive keyboard and a maximum 8.8 seconds of sampling time. It has three split points and a 2.8-inch disk drive.

The **Wersi MK1** features not only sampling, but Fourier and FM synthesis as well. It has 20 digital voices and can produce eight different sounds simultaneously. The MK1 stores 24 performance programs and 20 presets, plus cartridge memory. It has analog filtering, phasing, flanging, chorusing, stereo outputs, and a velocity- and pressure-sensitive, split keyboard which can layer up to four sounds.

From New England Digital, the **Synclavier** is a high-priced dream machine. Its computer is housed separately from the instrument itself. Partial timbres are constructed by additive synthesis, then combined to create sounds. The Synclavier is available in 8- to 128-voice versions, with a velocity- and pressure-sensitive keyboard and a 32-track sequencer. Sounds are stored on floppy disks or on one or more optional hard disk drives. Real time controllers include programmable left-hand wheels and a ribbon controller. A number of options are available, including sampling (with a 100 kHz sampling rate), music transcription, independent outputs for each channel, and a SMPTE reader.

The **Fairlight CMI** (Computer Musical Instrument) is one of Australia's leading exports. Sounds may be designed by Fourier synthesis and analysis, waveforms can be drawn on the monitor screen with a light pen, and samples may be resynthesized, edited, and spliced together. The CMI's 8-track sequencer can record in real time, or you can enter sequence data through the computer-type keyboard. Options include music transcription, a film music processor, and even a word processor. Like the Synclavier, the Fairlight's software is subject to frequent updates.

USED SYNTHESIZERS

If money's tight, or you don't think you really need all the very latest technical wizardry, you may consider purchasing a previously owned synthesizer. They're frequently available for less than half what they cost new, but be extremely careful. If you find one you like, check it out thoroughly, like a used car. Play it long enough to uncover any "ghosts in the machine." Does it stay in tune in every register? How long does it have to warm up? If it has pots, do they operate smoothly and without scratchiness? Do all the switches work? Is it too noisy when you play it? Do the oscillators bleed through even when they're supposed to be turned off? Does the keyboard trigger as it should, or does it occasionally glitch? If it has MIDI, will it work with equipment you already own or plan to buy?

Some problems can be fixed by a competent service technician, but it's going to cost extra. Besides, truly competent service technicians are hard to locate. For some instruments, it's next to impossible to find replacement parts. If you're stuck with an instrument that won't stay in tune from one octave to the next, or one that goes wacko every time you play middle C, you're going to be disillusioned with your purchase.

It's still quite possible to find an excellent older synth at a bargain price. If you're looking for a basic lead monosynth, you have a great number of choices. The

Minimoog was the first commercial instrument with pitch bend and modulation wheels. It features three oscillators with ranges from low-frequency to audio, two 3-stage envelope generators with a release bypass switch, and a generator for both pink and white noise (which can be used as a source of modulation). A good Minimoog has a classic sound and it's easy to play, even without patch memory.

The **ARP Odyssey** has sliders instead of knobs, and it's only a little more difficult to tune than a Minimoog. Though most models don't have a left-hand modulation controller, the Odyssey includes useful extras like ring modulation and a sample & hold which samples oscillator waveforms as well as pink and white noise. It can play two notes at the same time, but not two independent voices. There are at least five different versions of the Odyssey.

Another potential good buy is the **ARP 2600**. Introduced in 1970, it was the first portable synthesizer. It's hard-wired, but also uses patchcords for increased flexibility. The keyboard, which comes in its own case, was made in both monophonic and para-biphonic versions. The 2600 has three oscillators, a lowpass filter, white and pink noise, ADSR and AR envelopes, sample & hold, ring modulation, reverb, stereo outputs, two built-in speakers, and a voltage processor which can invert signals and introduce lag.

ARP also made the **Omni,** which became their best seller. The Omni II is a parapolyphonic instrument with three sections: bass, strings, and variable synth with one oscillator featuring sawtooth and square waveforms. The keyboard is split, so that the bass plays in the lower octave-and-a-half.

The **Polymoog** has a velocity-sensitive, split keyboard, three resonant filters, and eight variable preset patches. You can also program and recall two patches of your own design. Two master oscillators with sawtooth and variable pulse waveforms are divided into 71 tones. Each key has its own filter, amplifier, and envelope generator circuitry, making it possible to play up to 71 notes simultaneously.

The **Sequential Circuits Prophet-5** is an instrument which revolutionized polyphonic synthesis. Most instruments available today are variations on its design. The front panel lets you control five identical voices. It was the first synth from another company to adopt Moog-style pitch bend and modulation wheels, and the first with one-touch tuning. The later revisions memorize 120 patches. A unique scale mode can alter pitch relationships to achieve tunings other than equal temperament. If a monophonic synthesizer is what you need, the **Sequential Circuits Pro-One** has all the features of a single Prophet voice without program storage, with the addition of a built-in 40-note sequencer and an arpeggiator.

A more recent, more powerful Prophet synthesizer is the **Prophet-T8**, an 8-voice version with a 600-note sequencer and a keyboard that's both velocity- and pressure-sensitive. The weighted, wooden keyboard can be split at any point, assigning four voices to each side of the split. It weighs 60 pounds and stores 128 programs. The much less expensive **Prophet-600** is a 6-voice synth which memorizes 100 patches. The first MIDI instrument, it features an arpeggiator, real time sequencer, full control panel, and a numeric keypad for program selection, but no noise generator.

Moog's entry in the MIDI sweepstakes is the **Memorymoog Plus**, which features not two, but three oscillators per voice. It has six voices and recalls 100 programs through a calculator-like keypad. Operational modes, parameter information, and program numbers are displayed. The Memorymoog features sample & hold, an arpeggiator, and separate monophonic and polyphonic sequencers.

A great-sounding 2-voice instrument without user-programmable patch memory is the **Oberheim TVS-1**. It can play two different voices at the same time; the second voice comes in whenever more than one key is depressed, or they can be layered. The TVS-1 has a digitally-scanned keyboard, an analog sequencer, and sample & hold. It houses two Oberheim SEMs (**Synthesizer Expander Modules**), each of which is an independent synthesizer voice with its own controls. The SEM was originally designed with a built-in power supply to broaden the capabilities of almost any synthesizer. The **FVS-1** is the TVS-1's more popular big brother, with four SEMs for four completely different voices. Later models of the FVS were the first ready-made polysynths with microprocessor memory. The programmer module, which recalls 16 patches, contains an extra filter and a master LFO. Old Oberheim polyphonics were also made in 6- and 8-voice versions.

Oberheim later made the **OB-X**, their answer to the first Prophet. It was replaced by the **OB-Xa**, which features a split keyboard and memorizes 120 patch programs and eight keyboard split points. The OB-Xa comes in 4-, 6-, and 8-voice versions. The **Oberheim OB-8** has a programmable split keyboard, eight voices, and it also stores 120 patches. It has three LFOs with multiple waveforms plus noise and sample & hold. Modulation routing is extensive, and there's a choice of smooth or quantized portamento. The OB-8 also features two filter modes, an arpeggiator, several footswitch and pedal inputs, and stereo outputs.

Another early polysynth is the **Yamaha CS-80**, which plays eight simultaneous notes. Sixteen oscillators are divided into two independent channels for layering sounds. It comes with 22 factory-programmed presets, plus four banks of sliders for adjusting the parameters of four user-defined sounds, in addition to the main front panel sliders. The CS-80 features a force-sensitive keyboard, voltage-controlled highpass and lowpass filters, ring modulation, a pitch bend ribbon, and a chorus effect.

Glossary

AC coupling - method of transferring signals from one analog circuit to another, so that the AC portion of the signal is passed and the DC portion is suppressed

acoustic - pertaining to sound; a term describing mechanical vibrations in the audio range

additive synthesis - the construction of complex tones by combining simpler tones of various amplitudes and frequencies

ADSR - 1) four stages of an envelope: Attack, Decay, Sustain, Release; 2) a common type of four-stage envelope generator

aftertouch - pressure-sensitivity in a keyboard, also called force-sensitivity or second touch

algorithm - 1) a digital set of instructions for performing a function; 2) the configuration of operators in an FM digital synthesizer

aliasing - a type of noise generated by a digital sound source when a signal's frequency is greater than half the sampling rate

alignment - procedure for tuning or adjusting a circuit so that it exhibits specified operating characteristics

alphanumeric - consisting of letters and numbers

alternating current (AC) - a flow of electricity which periodically reverses direction

amplification - any means of increasing a signal's amplitude

amplifier - a circuit or device that can control the amplitude of a signal passing through it

amplitude - strength or intensity of a sound or signal; the measure of a current's deviation from its zero value

amplitude modulation (AM) - the use of a signal to change the amplitude of another signal

analog - 1) a term describing a circuit, device, or system which responds to continuously-variable parameters; 2) generated by hardware rather than by software

analog sequencer - a device which stores a series of control voltages for the purpose of playing back a sequence of events

analog synthesizer - 1) a synthesizer which is controlled primarily by voltages rather than by digital signals; a synthesizer which contains no digital circuitry; 2) loosely speaking, any synthesizer with hardware-based oscillators and filters

analog-to-digital (A/D) convertor - a circuit which periodically samples a voltage and generates a digital representation of its value

aperiodic - a term describing a phenomenon which doesn't repeat at regular intervals

AR generator - an envelope generator with two stages, Attack and Decay

arpeggiator - a synthesizer circuit or software which automatically plays arpeggios whenever two or more keys are depressed simultaneously

arpeggio - the playing of a chord or a group of notes as a succession of tones, rather than simultaneously

assignment priority - a keyboard logic system which determines how voices respond to keyboard depressions and in what order

attack - 1) the beginning of a sound or signal; 2) an envelope generator's first stage

attenuator - a control which can reduce the amplitude of signals passing through it

audio - within the range of frequencies normally heard by the human ear, commonly accepted as extending from approximately 20 Hz to 20 kHz

audio oscillator - a circuit or software which generates signals in the audio range

autoglide - a synthesizer function in which portamento is introduced whenever a key is depressed before the previous key has been released; also called automatic portamento or fingered portamento

autotune - automatic tuning; a function which digitally tunes all oscillators

balanced modulator - ring modulator

band - a range or region of frequencies between an upper and a lower limit

bandpass filter (BPF) - a circuit which passes only frequencies within a specified band, and attenuates frequencies above and below that band

band-reject filter (BRF) - a circuit which passes only frequencies above and below a specified band, and attenuates frequencies within that band; also called a bandstop filter

bandwidth - 1) the range of frequencies within a circuit's passband; 2) the range of frequencies a medium is capable of accurately reproducing

bank - a group of digital storage locations; a portion of digital memory

basic channel - the channel on which a MIDI transmitter sends in omni mode, usually channel 1 but often selectable

beat - a metronomic division which indicates rhythmic pulse and tempo

beats - periodic fluctuations in amplitude that occur when one signal is superimposed on another signal of related frequency

bend - to momentarily change a tone's pitch by means of a pitch bender; pitch bend

bias - a fixed value applied to a circuit to establish its operational reference point

biphonic - capable of playing two notes simultaneously; two-voice

bipolar - a term describing a potentiometer which may have either a positive or negative effect on the parameter being controlled

block diagram - a graphic representation of a patch, in which labeled rectangles representing circuits or functions are connected by lines or arrows representing how signals are routed

break point - 1) the starting note on a keyboard for boost or cut in the output or envelope, controlled by keyboard level or rate scaling; 2) an envelope level between the decay and sustain stages

buss - an electrical conductor which distributes or collects signals to or from several destinations or sources

calibration - process of comparing the operating characteristics of a circuit with a fixed standard and correcting any deviation

carrier - a signal which is modulated; modulation destination

CD-ROM - Compact Disk Read-Only Memory, a medium of storing digital information on a laser-encoded disk, which may not be altered or erased

cent - 1% of a semitone

center detent - a notch indicating the center position of a continuous controller or potentiometer

central processing unit (CPU) - the part of a computer which performs computations and follows the instructions contained in a program and in the computer's memory

chain - to link together patch programs or sequences in a particular order

chorusing - a time-delay effect which "thickens" the signal being processed, sometimes creating the illusion of more instruments

Chroma interface - a proprietary, 8-bit parallel interface found on Chroma synthesizers, made by Fender Musical Instruments

chromatic - divided by semitones

circuit - a configuration of electronic components which fulfills a deliberate function

clangorous - term describing a sound consisting of non-harmonic overtones

click track - one track of a multitrack tape recording on which a metronomic pulse or another audible sync signal is recorded for the purpose of synchronizing subsequent tracks

clipping - audible distortion of a signal output, caused by overloading a circuit or transducer

clock - an oscillator or software which generates periodic pulses, used to maintain synchronization or trigger events

coarse tune - a wide-range potentiometer for tuning an analog oscillator to roughly within a desired range

continuous controller - a physical device for controlling certain synthesizer parameters, such as a pitch bender or foot pedal

continuously variable - a term describing the ability of a circuit or a control to be changed by any degree within its range, and at any time; not quantized

contour - a sound or signal's dynamic variations in amplitude or spectrum; envelope

contour generator - envelope generator

control input - the input to a circuit which accepts a control signal to modify that circuit's operating characteristics

controller - a device which can produce a change in one or more parameters, and which can be directly operated or programmed by the synthesist

control voltage (CV) - an analog electrical signal produced by one circuit which determines the operating characteristics of another circuit or circuits

cross modulation (x-mod) - the use of an audio signal to change the frequency and/or spectrum of another signal; also called linear FM

current - the flow of electrons through a conductor, measured in amperes

cutoff frequency (Fc) - the point at which a filter begins to attenuate the spectrum of a signal passing through it; also called corner frequency

cycle - a complete wave; the basic unit of oscillation

DCB - Digital Control Bus, a proprietary interface found on some Roland instruments and sequencers

DC coupling - a method of transferring signals down to 0 Hz from one analog circuit to another

decay - 1) the portion of a sound or signal in which its amplitude, pitch, or brightness decreases; 2) an ADSR generator's second stage

decibel (dB) - the standard unit for measuring loudness; the ratio between a sound or signal's amplitude or power and a reference level

default - term describing a value which is selected unless otherwise specified

delay - 1) delay line; 2) vibrato delay

delay line - a signal processing device that introduces a time delay between its input and its output

detune - to offset the frequency of one oscillator in relation to another

diagnostics - a procedure for circuit calibration, alignment, and adjustment

digital - a term describing a circuit, device, or system which represents variable quantities by numerical patterns; that which uses data in discrete steps, rather than continuously variable quantities; computer-based

digital control - a system wherein the signals produced by a computer determine the operating characteristics of other circuits

digital delay - a microprocessor-controlled delay line

digitally-controlled amplifier (DCA) - an amplifier whose gain is controlled by signals from a microprocessor

digitally-controlled oscillator (DCO) - an oscillator whose frequency is controlled by signals from a microprocessor

digitally-controlled wave (DCW) - in phase distortion synthesis, a modulating signal which affects another signal's spectrum

digital oscillator - a software-generated source of audio signals

digital sequencer - a device, circuit, or software which digitally stores and plays back performance information

digital-to-analog convertor (DAC) - a circuit which generates analog voltages which correspond to digital signals present at its input

digitized - converted to or stored in digital form

DIN connector - a standard, 5-pin electrical connector, specified for use in MIDI hardware

direct current (DC) - electrical flow in only one direction

disk drive - a device for transferring digital information to and from a computer disk

display - a device for viewing alphanumeric and/or graphic information, such as an LCD or a computer monitor screen

distortion - inaccurate reproduction of a waveform

Doppler effect - the apparent shift in frequency that occurs when a sound source is in motion relative to its point of perception

double manual - a term describing an instrument with two keyboards

double mode - a state in which two sounds can be played simultaneously with each key; layering

drift - to unintentionally deviate from an assigned value

dump - to transfer data from one medium to another, as from synthesizer memory to external storage

duophonic - biphonic; two-voice

duty cycle - the positive portion of a complete pulse wave; pulse width

dynamics - variations in sound over its duration; changes related to time

echo - a discrete repetition of a sound or signal

edit - 1) to make changes in patch parameters recalled from memory; 2) to alter sequence information

edit mode - a state which allows the synthesist to alter programmed patch parameters

emphasis - intensification of a harmonic component; resonance

envelope - a sound or signal's dynamic variations in amplitude or spectrum from its beginning until its end; a sound event's contour

envelope follower - a circuit which generates a control signal proportional to the amplitude of a signal input, often used to duplicate the envelope of an external audio signal

envelope generator (EG) - a circuit or software which generates a changing control signal in discrete stages, most often used to control the dynamic output of an amplifier or filter; also called contour generator or transient generator

envelope tracking - a function in which envelope parameters are varied in relation to the location of the depressed keys; also called key follow

EPROM - electrically-programmable read-only memory; ROM which may be permanently altered

equalization (EQ) - any deliberate alteration of a sound or signal's frequency spectrum or bandwidth, often by means of an equalizer

equalizer - a circuit or device used to alter a sound or signal's spectrum

equal-tempered - conforming to an intonation system wherein the octave is divided into 12 equal intervals; well-tempered

exponential - a relationship in which a change in one value causes a proportional change in another value

feedback - routing part of a circuit's signal output back to its input; regeneration (in phase) or degeneration (out of phase)

filter - a circuit which alters a signal's frequency content by attenuating selected portions

filter modulation - the use of a signal to change filter frequency

filter sweep - a slow change in a filter's cutoff frequency

fine tune - a narrow-range pot for tuning an analog oscillator with greater accuracy than with a coarse tuning pot

fingered portamento - a synthesizer function in which portamento takes effect whenever a key is depressed before the previous key is released; autoglide

first-note priority - a system found on keyboards which play only the first notes depressed, so that no other voices sound after the maximum number of keys is held down

flanger - a signal processor which delays a signal, and by mixing the direct and delayed signals, causes reinforcement and cancellation of various harmonic components

floppy disk - a flexible circle of magnetic material, usually enclosed in a square, cardboard or plastic sleeve, which stores digital data in the form of charged particles; a digital storage medium

FM synthesis - a method of generating complex waveforms by modulating the frequencies of sine waves with other sine waves

footage - a division of frequency ranges by octaves, derived from the lengths of organ pipes

force-sensitive - a term describing a keyboard which responds to how hard a key is depressed after it's down; also called pressure-sensitive, aftertouch, or second touch

formant - a resonant peak in a sound's frequency spectrum

four-pole filter - a filter with a -24 dB/octave rolloff

frequency - the number of periodic cycles in a given length of time, usually measured in cycles per second (Hertz); the rate of vibration, which determines pitch

frequency modulation (FM) - the use of a signal to change another signal's frequency

frequency shifter - a circuit or device which changes each of a waveform's component frequencies to an equal degree

FSK - Frequency Shift Keying, a means of synchronization in which two audio frequencies alternate at a basic clock rate

function - 1) in Yamaha synthesizers, a set of performance parameters such as modulation depth, pitch bend range, and portamento mode; 2) the purpose for which a circuit or software is designed

function generator- a circuit which generates waveforms either one at a time or periodically; what some synthesizer builders call an envelope generator and others call an oscillator

fundamental - the primary frequency of a sound or signal; a complex waveform's lowest harmonic component; the first harmonic, also called fundamental frequency

gain - the ratio between the amplitude of a circuit's input signal and the amplitude of its output, usually expressed in dB

gain factor - the factor by which a circuit amplifies an input signal

gate - an on/off signal generated by a controller, used to define an event's duration; a signal which indicates whether a key is depressed

glide - an effect in which pitch slides smoothly up or down; portamento

glissando (gliss) - an effect in which pitch changes in discrete, chromatic steps; quantized portamento

graphic equalizer - a circuit or device in which the amplitude of various bands of the frequency spectrum are independently altered using linear potentiometers

hardware - mechanical, electrical, or electronic instruments, devices, or systems; instruments or equipment, as opposed to software

hard-wired - term describing an electronic instrument with inflexible signal routing incorporated in its design; normalized

harmonic - a frequency component of a complex waveform which is a whole-number multiple of the fundamental frequency

harmonic contour - a sound or signal's dynamic variations in spectrum; also called filter envelope or timbral envelope

harmony - the simultaneous occurrence of two or more musical sounds, or their relationship; the vertical structure of music

Hertz (Hz) - cycles per second, the standard unit of frequency

high-note priority - a system found on keyboards which play only the highest keys depressed when the maximum number is held down

highpass filter (HPF) - a circuit which passes only frequencies above its cutoff frequency, and attenuates those below that point

hold - a synthesizer function which causes notes or chords to continue indefinitely, even when the keys are released; a type of latching

hybrid - 1) a design whose origin is a combination of dissimilar designs; 2) an instrument with both analog and digital circuitry; a term which generally refers to a digitally-controlled analog synthesizer

impedance - a circuit's opposition to the flow of alternating current, measured in Ohms

increment - quantity of increase or decrease

initial cutoff frequency - the cutoff frequency of a filter when the value of its control input is zero

initial decay - the time its takes an envelope to fall from its peak to its sustain level; the second stage of an ADSR generator

initial gain - the gain of an amplifier when the value of its control input is zero

intensity - the strength, loudness, or amplitude of a sound or signal

interface - a means of connecting two instruments or devices, allowing them to exchange information

interval - the difference between two musical pitches

inverter- a circuit or software which reverses the positive and negative portions of a signal, changing its polarity

jack - a socket into which a corresponding plug can be inserted, which serves as the input or output port of a circuit, instrument, or device

joystick - a continuous controller, consisting of a lever which can be moved on a circular axis, and which may control two or more functions simultaneously

keyboard - 1) a controller which provides synthesizer circuitry with signals defining pitch and rhythm, by means of depressing keys; the primary tactile interface between a keyboard instrument and a performer;

2) a typewriter-style device for entering alphanumeric data into a computer

keyboard logic - the software which determines the operating priorities of an electronic keyboard

keyboard tracking - a function in which filter frequency is varied in relation to the location of depressed keys

key follow - a function in which envelope parameters are varied in relation to the location of the depressed keys; also called envelope tracking

kiloHertz (kHz) - a standard unit of frequency, equal to 1000 Hz

lag - a function which retards changes from one value to another

last-note priority - a system found on keyboards which play only the most recent notes depressed when the maximum number is held down

latching - a function which memorizes instantaneous parameters, such as which keys were most recently depressed

layering - a synthesizer mode which allows two or more sounds to be played simultaneously with each key; doubling

legato - a term which describes a musical passage played with no perceptible interruption between successive notes

level - amplitude or intensity of a signal

LFO mod - modulation in which a low frequency oscillator is the control source

linear - a relationship in which a change in one value causes an equivalent change in another value

linear FM - cross-modulation of oscillator frequency by another oscillator, in which the modulating oscillator maintains a constant frequency

link - a patch program which may be played at the same time as another program, as in patch layering or keyboard splitting

load - to transfer data from one medium to another, as from external memory to a synthesizer's program banks, or from disk to RAM

location modulation - any deliberate change in the perceived location of a sound source

lookup table - digitally-stored information which contains the numbers needed to synthesize waveforms; also called a wavetable

loudness - a subjective measure of the ear's sensitivity to the amplitude or intensity of any sound

loudness contour - 1) a sound's dynamic variations in intensity; amplitude envelope; 2) variations of the ear's sensitivity in relation to pitch

loudspeaker - a transducer which converts electrical signals into sound

low-frequency - below the range of normal human hearing; sub-audio

low-frequency oscillator (LFO) - a circuit or software which generates periodic signals in the sub-audio range, most often used as a modulation source; also called modulation generator or sweep

low-note priority - a system found on keyboards which play only the lowest keys depressed after the maximum number is held down

lowpass filter (LPF) - an circuit which passes only frequencies below its cutoff frequency and attenuates those above that point; the most common type of synthesizer filter

manual control - directly adjusting analog synthesizer parameters by hand, as opposed to voltage control

master - an instrument or device which controls other instruments or devices (slaves) in a system

master incremental controller - a knob or slider used to vary the values of every programmable synthesizer parameter

matrix panel - a modular panel on which a number of pin matrices are installed, used to connect various circuits

memory - 1) a medium of storing information; 2) a circuit which contains digitally-recorded information

microprocessor - a computer processor enclosed in a microchip

MIDI - Musical Instrument Digital Interface; a means of communication between instruments or devices

MIDI box - a device for combining, rerouting, or altering MIDI information

MIDI cable - a shielded, twisted pair electrical cable, 50 feet or less, terminated on each end by a 5-pin DIN male plug, with the conductors connected to pins 4 and 5 and the shield connected to pin 2 at both ends

MIDI In - an opto-isolated, female DIN jack which receives MIDI information

MIDI Out - a female DIN jack which transmits MIDI data

MIDI Thru - a female DIN jack which transfers MIDI data present at the corresponding MIDI IN

millisecond (mS) - 1/1000th of a second

mini-keyboard - 1) a musical keyboard which is scaled down to a smaller-than-standard size; 2) an instrument with such a keyboard

mixer - a circuit, software, or device which can add two or more signal inputs into a common signal output, and which usually lets you control the gain of each input as well as the output

mode - a condition which determines how something may function; status; a state of being

modular synthesizer - a system comprised of various semi-independent circuits which can be interconnected by patchcords for the production of electronic music

modulation - any perceptible change in a sound or signal's character in response to a control signal

modulation controller - a specialized device which varies the depth of one circuit's effect on another circuit's parameters; a continuous controller which can govern synthesizer vibrato depth, usually operated by the performer's left hand

modulation generator (MG) - a low-frequency oscillator

module - a self-contained device, instrument, circuit, or collection of circuits which can be interconnected with other modules to form a complete system

mono mode - a MIDI mode which restricts the assignment of voices to one voice per channel

monophonic - capable of playing only one note at a time; one-voice

monosynth - a monophonic synthesizer

multimode filter - 1) a filter which combines lowpass and highpass circuitry for a variety of possible passbands and stopbands; 2) a state-variable filter

multiple trigger - a keyboard system in which a trigger appears at the beginning of each key depression, regardless of whether any other keys are depressed

multi-timbral - term describing a synthesizer which is capable of producing a number of dissimilar sounds simultaneously; also called polytimbral

multitrack - 1) a process by which independent signals are recorded on multiple tracks of magnetic tape or in digital memory, so you can monitor previously-recorded material while recording (overdubbing) additional material; 2) term describing a tape recorder, sequencer, or computer software which performs multitrack recording

musique concrete - music which incorporates sounds traditionally considered non-musical; music constructed from recorded materials

natural harmonic series - the mathematical relationship which exists among the harmonic components of musical sounds; a profile of pitches or frequencies which are whole-number multiples of a fundamental pitch or frequency

negative sawtooth - a sawtooth wave which begins at its peak instantaneous amplitude and then descends to zero

noise - 1) a random or semi-random distribution of all audible frequencies; 2) an undesirable component of audio signals generated by the sound source, including hiss, hum, distortion, aliasing, and rumble

noise gate - an amplifier which closes whenever the input signal drops below a specified level or threshold

noise generator - a circuit or software which generates aperiodic waveforms, usually pink or white noise

noise reduction - a device or system to improve signal-to-noise ratio

non-volatile - term which describes an information storage medium which retains its memory even when its power supply is turned off

notch filter - a band-reject filter with a narrow stopband

Note Off - a MIDI signal which indicates the beginning of an envelope's release stage

Note On - a MIDI signal which indicates the beginning of an envelope's attack

Nyquist rate - the highest frequency at which a sampled sound is accurately reproduced, equal to half the sampling rate

octave - the interval between two pitches when one is twice the frequency of the other; an interval of 12 semitones

Ohm - the resistance of a circuit through which one volt maintains a current of one ampere; the standard unit of measuring a circuit's opposition to current flow

omni mode - a MIDI mode in which all instruments in a system respond to all channels; the power-up condition of instruments conforming strictly to MIDI specifications

operator - a software-generated pairing of a sine wave and an envelope controlling its amplitude, used in FM synthesis

oscillator - a circuit or software which generates periodic waveforms; a synthesizer's primary source of pitched sound

oscillator sync - a function which synchronizes the phase relationship of two oscillators, so that one is phase-locked to the other

oscilloscope - an electronic test instrument which visually displays waveforms

outboard - term which describes a device which is external to the primary instrument, such as a self-contained sequencer or a signal processing device; peripheral

overdrive - intentional distortion of an audio waveform, usually created by overloading an amplifier circuit

overdub - to record audio or performance information in synchronization with previously-recorded information, either on magnetic media (such as recording tape) or in digital memory

overtone - a component of a complex waveform which has a frequency higher than the fundamental frequency; also called a partial

page - a configuration or mode in which a group of synthesizer front panel controls assume a particular set of functions

parallel interface - a connection between instruments or devices in which several bits (usually a byte) of digital information are transferred simultaneously over multiple pin connections

parameter - a variable quality or quantity which contributes to the whole

parameter display - a device which indicates the value of a parameter to be viewed or edited

parametric equalizer - a circuit or device which can add peaks or dips to a system's frequency bandwidth by selecting a center frequency, bandwidth, and amount of harmonic boost or cut

parapolyphonic - term which describes a synthesizer or keyboard which can sound a number of notes, but cannot trigger individual envelopes simultaneously, such as an ARP Omni

partial - component of a complex waveform which has a frequency higher than the fundamental frequency; overtone

passband - the range of frequencies which a circuit passes unattenuated

patch - 1) a collection of parameters which defines a synthesized sound; 2) to temporarily connect various circuits and/or specify synthesizer parameters for the purpose of constructing a particular sound

patchcord - a length of electrical cable with plugs at either end, used to connect two instruments, modules, devices, or circuits

patch librarian - a personal computer program which lets you store and recall synthesizer patch programs

patch program - a memorized set of parameters which defines a synthesized sound; also called a patch, a program, and sometimes a voice

periodic - term describing a phenomena which repeats itself with regularity

phase - 1) the position of a wave in time; 2) the instantaneous relationship between two waves

phase angle - the degree of a wave's completion at any given point

phase cancellation - the attenuation which occurs when two simultaneous waves are of related frequency and different polarity

phase distortion - a method of digital synthesis in which a new waveform is produced by changing the phase angles of an oscillator waveform

phase modulation - a deliberate change in the phase of a sound or signal

phaser - a signal-processing device which passes an audio signal through an allpass filter, and by mixing the original signal with the filtered signal, changes its spectral phase relationships; phase shifter

phase shift - the angular displacement of two simultaneous waves of related frequency

phrasing - 1) the manner in which the audible details of musical performance are executed; 2) in performance, how a performer separates groups of notes within a melodic line

pink noise - a random distribution of all audible frequencies, in which every octave has equal amplitude

pin matrix - an electrical grid into which pins are placed to connect various circuits

pitch - the quality of a musical tone which is determined by its fundamental frequency; the position of a tone in a musical scale

pitch bend - a process in which one momentarily raises or lowers oscillator frequency by a desired amount, often using a specialized continuous controller

pitch shifter - a signal processing device which changes an audio signal's pitch while maintaining its harmonic spectrum; also called a harmonizer

pitch-to-MIDI convertor - a circuit or device which produces MIDI signals corresponding to the frequency of a signal input

pitch-to-voltage convertor - a circuit or device which produces control voltages proportional to the frequency of a signal input

play mode - a mode in which a sequencer can play back a recorded performance

poly-mod - polyphonic modulation of an audio oscillator or filter by another oscillator or an envelope generator

poly mode - a MIDI mode in which channels respond polyphonically

polyphonic - term describing a musical instrument which can produce more than one independent tone simultaneously; multi-voice

polysynth - a polyphonic synthesizer

portamento - a continuous transition from one pitch to another; glide

positive sawtooth - a sawtooth wave which ascends to its peak instantaneous amplitude and then instantly drops to zero

potentiometer (pot) - a variable resistor, often used to manually adjust signal levels, parameter values, or other quantities

preprogrammed - term which describes a synthesizer which has patches programmed by the manufacturer stored in its memory; factory-programmed

preset - 1) a hard-wired patch which cannot be permanently altered by the user; 2) patch program

pressure-sensitive - term describing a keyboard which responds to how hard a key is depressed after it's down; also called force-sensitive, aftertouch, or second touch

priority - a system which determines what notes will sound if more than the maximum number of keys are depressed, and in what order

program - 1) to determine patch parameters; 2) to store patch parameters in digital memory;

3) a memorized set of patch parameters or operating instructions; 4) computer software; 5) to write computer software

program chain - a set of patch programs which may be stepped through sequentially

programmable - term describing a synthesizer which can memorize and recall patch parameters

program display - a visual representation of digitally stored information, usually the name or number assigned to a selected patch program

pulse wave - a waveform characterized by two abrupt changes in instantaneous amplitude; a rectangular wave

pulse width (PW) - the proportion of a complete pulse wave possessing a positive value; duty cycle

pulse width modulation (PWM) - any change in a signal's duty cycle caused by a control signal

Q - resonance

quantization - the process of dividing a set of values into incremental steps

quantization noise - the noise which occurs when a signal is converted to digital form; digital noise

RAM - random access memory, the temporary portion of computer memory which lets you enter and retrieve information in any order

RAM cartridge - a device for storing digital information which may be entered or altered by the user

ramp wave - a sawtooth wave

real time mode - a mode in which a sequencer records note data, and possibly other performance data, exactly as it is played

rectangular wave - a pulse wave

regeneration - routing a filter's signal output back to its input; also called resonance or positive feedback

release - 1) the final stage of a synthesizer envelope, which occurs when a Note Off command is received or the gate is withdrawn; 2) a sound's final decay

release velocity - the rate at which a key is released

remote keyboard - a self-contained musical keyboard, independent of the sound-producing electronics of an instrument, used to control separate instruments or modules

resistance - a circuit's opposition to electrical flow, measured in Ohms

resonance - 1) an increase in the gain of a signal at the filter cutoff frequency, produced by regenerating a portion of the filter's output; also called filter emphasis, regeneration, or Q; 2) the tendency of a circuit or an object to exhibit increased gain at a particular frequency or frequencies

reverberation (reverb) - 1) acoustical reflection; 2) a signal processing circuit or device which simulates acoustical reflection

ribbon controller - a device for changing oscillator frequency by placing one's finger on its surface and sliding it up or down

ring modulation - amplitude modulation in which an amplifier's output is equal to the sums and differences of the program and the carrier; balanced modulation

rolloff - the rate of attenuation above or below a filter's cutoff frequency, measured in decibels per octave; filter slope

ROM - read-only memory, the portion of computer memory which is permanently stored in circuits, usually containing information necessary to the computer's operation

ROM cartridge - a device which contains digital information which may not be changed

sample - 1) to measure or quantize an instantaneous value; 2) to digitally encode an analog signal; 3) a digitally-recorded sound

sample & hold (S/H) - a circuit which, on command, samples a continuously variable signal input and holds its output at that level until the next sampling command; a synthesizer circuit most often used to produce random signals

sampler - a musical instrument, processing device, or computer software capable of digitally recording and manipulating sound

sampling rate - the frequency at which a sampled waveform is quantized

sampling keyboards - keyboard instruments capable of recording and manipulating sound

sawtooth wave - a waveform which contains every component of the natural harmonic series; a ramp wave

scale mode - a function found on some synthesizers, which allows individual tuning of each scale division

scaling - a function found on some synthesizers, which allows the user to alter pitch relationships within a scale, allowing tunings other than equal temperament

scroll - to move information being displayed on a monitor screen so that a different part of it is visible

second touch - pressure sensitivity

self-oscillation - the result of extreme filter regeneration, in which a filter generates a sine wave at its cutoff frequency

semitone - the interval between two adjacent keys; a half step

sequence - 1) a series of voltages or keystroke commands; 2) a musical performance recorded on a digital sequencer

sequencer - a circuit, device, or software which records and stores performance information so that it may reproduce the performance; a sequence recorder

serial interface - a connection between instruments or devices in which digital information is transferred one bit at a time

sidebands - a range of frequencies generated when an audio signal modulates another; sum and difference tones

signal - an electrical impulse

signal processor - a circuit or device (such as an equalizer or delay line) which modifies some audible characteristic of a signal input

signal-to-noise (S/N) ratio - the difference between a signal level and the level of unintentional noise produced by a circuit, device, or system, expressed in decibels

sine wave - a pure, simple waveform, comprised of one frequency with no overtones; a single harmonic component

single-step mode - a mode in which a sequencer records note data, and possibly other performance data, one event at a time; step time

single trigger - a keyboard system in which a trigger appears at the beginning of a key depression only when no other keys are depressed

slave - an instrument or device being controlled by another instrument or device (the master) in a system

slope - the degree of filter rolloff, expressed in decibels per octave

SMPTE code - a synchronization protocol, developed by NASA and adapted by the Society of Motion Picture and Television Engineers, which divides time into hours, minutes, seconds, frames, and subframes

software - information which may be used or accessed by hardware

song - 1) a collection of sequences which may be played back in a particular order; 2) a complete multitrack sequence

song position pointer - a MIDI message which indicates how many MIDI clocks have passed at any point in a sequence; also called song pointer

sound wave - a single, audible fluctuation of barometric pressure caused by a vibrating object

spectrum - a sound or signal's total harmonic content

spectral display - a graphic representation of a waveform's spectrum

split keyboard - a musical keyboard which can be electronically divided into two or more sections, each controlling a different sound or function

split point - the point at which a keyboard is split

square wave - a pulse wave with a 50% duty cycle, comprised of odd harmonics only

staccato - a term which describes a musical passage played with distinct breaks between successive notes; playing only a short portion of a note's full value, the rest of which is replaced by a rest

staircase wave - a quantized sawtooth wave

state-variable filter - a filter which combines response characteristics for a variety of possible passbands and stopbands; a multi-mode filter

step time - a means of recording sequencer data one event at a time, as opposed to real time

stopband - the range of frequencies which a filter attenuates

stop mode - a mode in which a sequencer stops playing a recorded performance

string synthesizer - an electronic keyboard instrument whose primary purpose is the imitation of orchestral stringed instruments

sub-audio - below the range of frequencies normally heard by the human ear; low frequency

sub-octave - a frequency which is one or two octaves below another frequency

sub-oscillator - a divider circuit which generates a sub-octave of an oscillator signal

subtractive synthesis - the process of producing tone colors by filtering complex waveforms

sum and difference tones - sidebands produced when one audio signal modulates another, and whose frequencies are the mathematical sums and differences of all harmonic components

sustain - the portion of an envelope in which amplitude or brightness remains at a constant level; an ADSR generator's third stage

sweep - 1) low frequency oscillator; 2) to gradually change a frequency or waveform

switch trigger - a control signal which indicates the beginning of an envelope by a sudden, momentary drop in voltage, used by Moog synthesizers; a negative trigger

sync - 1) a function which synchronizes the phase of one oscillator signal with another; 2) to make instruments or devices operate in tandem, or simultaneous performances occur with identical timing; synchronization

sync sweep - an effect in which an oscillator's frequency is swept while the oscillator is phase-locked to another oscillator, resulting in waveform modulation rather than frequency modulation

sync track - a recording of a reference signal used to synchronize instruments, devices, or performances

synthesizer - a musical instrument, comprised of various circuits which generate and modify electrical signals so that they may be converted to sound

system common - certain MIDI messages transmitted to all instruments in a system, such as song pointer, song select, and tune request

system exclusive - MIDI messages addressed to instruments from a particular manufacturer and ignored by other instruments in a system

system real-time - MIDI messages which are used to synchronize all instruments in a system

system reset - a MIDI message which returns all instruments in a system to their power-up condition

tempo tap - a feature found on some instruments which changes clock rate in response to footswitch depressions

thumbwheel - a continuous controller which is rolled on its axis to control a specific function, most often used to control pitch bend or modulation depth

timbre - tone color, which is dependent on harmonic content and distinguishes one sound from another

touch sensitive - a term describing a keyboard which responds to the velocity or force with which it's played

track - 1) to accurately respond to another circuit's control output; 2) a single recorded performance on a multitrack tape or in a multitrack sequencer

transducer - a device which converts energy from one form to another, such as a microphone, which converts acoustical energy into electrical energy

transients - harmonic components which appear only during the attack of a sound or signal

transpose - to play a musical passage or composition in a different key; to change key signature

tremolo - low-frequency amplitude modulation of an audio signal; periodic variation of a sound's intensity at a rate of approximately 5 - 10 Hz

triangle wave - a waveform with a strong fundamental and weak overtones, comprised of odd-numbered harmonics only

trigger - a control signal which indicates the beginning of an event, usually the beginning of an envelope

trill - a musical embellishment in which two pitches alternate at an approximate rate of 5 - 10 Hz; low-frequency square wave modulation of an audio frequency

truncate - to shorten a recorded sample by cutting off or removing a portion

two-pole filter - a filter with a -12 db/octave rolloff

unipolar - a term describing a potentiometer which changes a parameter from zero value to a positive value

unison - the interval between two identical pitches

unison mode - a keyboard mode in which all voices are assigned to each key depression

unity - the gain of an amplifier when the output is equal to the input

user-friendly - technically comprehensible without difficulty; easily understood by the average person

user-programmable - term describing a synthesizer which can memorize patch parameters determined by the programmer or performer

variable - a value which can be changed

VCA - voltage controlled amplifier; an amplifier whose gain may be determined by a control voltage

VCF - voltage controlled filter; a filter whose cutoff frequency may be determined by a control voltage

VCO - voltage controlled oscillator; an oscillator whose frequency (and possibly waveform) may be determined by a control voltage

velocity-sensitive - term describing a keyboard which responds to how quickly its keys are struck, and sometimes how quickly they are released

verify - to run a procedure which indicates that a data transfer was successful

vibrato - sub-audio frequency modulation of an audio signal by a sine or triangle wave; periodic variation in pitch at a rate of approximately 5 - 10 Hz

vibrato delay - a circuit which introduces a time delay between a trigger or Note On command and the onset of vibrato

vocoder - a device which divides the dynamic spectrum of an audio signal input into multiple bands and imparts that dynamic spectrum to another audio signal; often used to make synthesizers "talk"

voice - in a synthesizer, the output of an independent audio signal path

volatile memory - digital memory which is lost when its power supply is interrupted

voltage - electromotive force, expressed in volts

voltage control - a system wherein the analog electrical signals produced by certain circuits control the operating characteristics of other circuits

voltage pedal - a foot pedal which puts out a control voltage which is proportional to the angle of its treadle

voltage trigger - a control signal which indicates the beginning of an envelope by a sudden, momentary rise in voltage

wave - a complete cycle; a sound or signal's instantaneous changes in amplitude during one cycle

waveform - 1) a sound or signal; 2) the shape of an individual wave; the instantaneous amplitude versus time characteristics of a sound or signal

waveform modulation - any deliberate change in the shape, and thus the spectrum, of a waveform, especially in response to a control signal

wavetable - a set of digitally-stored numbers which define the parameters of a waveform; a lookup table

wheel - thumbwheel

white noise - a random distribution of all audible frequencies, each with equal amplitude

CONTACTS

Akai Professional Products
P. O. Box 2344
Fort Worth, TX 76113

Apple Computer
20235 Mariani Avenue
Cupertino, CA 95014

Atari Corporation
Box 61657
Sunnyvale, CA 94088

Big Briar, Inc.
Box 869
Natick, MA 01760

Casio, Inc.
Elec. Musical Inst. Div.
15 Gardner Road
Fairfield, NJ 07006

Commodore/Amiga
983 University
Los Gatos, CA 95030

Commodore
1200 Wilson Drive
West Chester, PA 19380

Computers & Music
1989 Junipero Serra Blvd.
Daly City, CA 94014

J. L. Cooper Electronics
1931 Pontius Avenue
West Los Angeles, CA
90025

Decillionix
P. O. Box 70985
Sunnyvale, CA 94086

Digidesign
920 Commercial
Palo Alto, CA 94303

Dr. T's Music Software
66 Louise Road
Chesnut Hill, MA 02167

E-mu Systems, Inc.
1600 Green Hills Road
Scotts Valley, CA 95066

Ensoniq Corporation
263 Great Valley Parkway
Malvern, PA 19355

Europa Technology
1638 W. Washington Blvd.
Venice, CA 90291

Fairlight Instruments, Inc.
2945 Westwood Blvd.
Los Angeles, CA 90064

Fender Musical Instruments
1130 Columbia Street
Brea, CA 92621

Garfield Electronics
Box 1941
Burbank, CA 91507

Hybrid Arts Inc.
11920 W. Olympic Blvd.
Los Angeles, CA 90064

IBM
Box 1328
Boca Raton, FL 33429

Indus Systems
9304 Deering Avenue
Chatsworth, CA 91311

Kaman Music Distributors
(Seiko)
P. O. Box 507
Bloomfield, CT 06002

Kawai America Corporation
P. O. Box 438
24200 S. Vermont Avenue
Harbor City, CA 90710

Korg U.S.A.
89 Frost Street
Westbury, NY 11590

Kurzweil Music Systems
411 Waverley Oaks Road
Waltham, MA 02154-8464

Mark of the Unicorn
222 Third Street
Cambridge, MA 02142

Mellotron
36 Main Street
Port Washington, NY 11050

Micro Music
210-C Marray Drive
Atlanta, GA 30341

Mimetics Coporation
P. O. Box 60238, Station A
Palo Alto, CA 94306

Moog Music & Electronics
2500 Walden Avenue
Buffalo, NY 14225

MusicData Inc.
8444 Wilshire Blvd.
Beverly Hills, CA 90211

MusicNet
P.O. Box 274
Beekman, NY 12570

New England Digital
Box 546
White River Junction, VT
05001

Oberheim
11650 W. Olympic Blvd.
Los Angeles, CA 90064

On-Site Music Group (Siel)
3000 Marcus Avenue
Lake Success, NY 11042

Opcode Systems
707 Urban Lane
Palo Alto, CA 94301

PAIA Electronics, Inc.
1020 W. Wilshire Blvd.
Oklahoma City, OK 73116

Passport Designs
625 Miramontes Street
Half Moon Bay, CA 94109

PAN Network
P.O. Box 162
Skippack, PA 19474

Personal Composer
PO Box 648
Honaunau, HI 96726

RolandCorp US
7200 Dominion Circle
Los Angeles, CA 90040

Sequential
3051 North First Street
San Jose, CA 95134

Sonus
21430 Strathern St., Suite H
Canoga Park, CA 91304

Southworth Music Systems
91 Ann Lee Road
Harvard, MA 01451

Synchronous Technologies
Box 14467
1020 W. Wilshire Blvd.
Oklahoma City, OK 73113

Syntech Corporation
5699 Kanan Road
Agoura, CA 91301

360 Systems
18730 Oxnard Street
Tarzana, CA 91356

Wersi Electronics
1720 Hempstead Road
P. O. Box 5318
Lancaster, PA 17601

Yamaha International Corp.
Professional Products Div.
P. O. Box 6600
Buena Park, CA 90622

BIBLIOGRAPHY

Aftertouch, P.O. Box 2338, Northridge, CA 91323-2338

Craig Anderton, **MIDI for Musicians**, Music Sales, 24 E. 22nd St., New York, NY 10010

Jon Appleton and Ronald Perera, **The Development & Practice of Electronic Music**, Greenwood, 88 Post Rd. W., Box 5007, Westport, CT 06881

Hal Chamberlin, **Musical Applications of Microprocessors**, Hayden Book Co., Hasbrouck Heights, NJ

Computer Music Journal, MIT Press, 28 Carleton St., Cambridge, MA 02142

Dave Crombie, **The Synthesizer & Electronic Keyboard Handbook**, Alfred A. Knopf, 201 E. 50th St., New York, NY 10022

Tom Darter and Greg Armbruster, Editors, **The Art of Electronic Music**, Wm. Morrow & Co., 105 Madison Ave., New York, NY 10016

Herbert Deutsch, **Synthesis**, Alfred Publishing, Sherman Oaks, CA

Devarahi, **The Complete Guide to Synthesizers**, Prentice-Hall, Englewood Cliffs, NJ 07632

Electronic Musician, Mix Publications, Inc., 2608 Ninth St., Berkeley, CA 94710

The IMA Bulletin, International MIDI Association, 11857 Hartsook St., North Hollywood, CA 91607

Keyboard Magazine, 20085 Stevens Creek, Cupertino, CA 95014-9967

Max Mathews, **The Technology of Computer Music**, MIT Press, Cambridge, 28 Carleton St., Cambridge, MA 02142

MIDI Specification 1.0, International MIDI Association, 11857 Hartsook St., North Hollywood, CA 91607

Curtis Roads, Editor, **Composers and the Computer**, Wm. Kaufmann, Inc., 95 First St., Los Altos, CA 94022

Curtis Roads & John Strawn, Editors, **Foundations of Computer Music**, MIT Press, 28 Carleton St., Cambridge, MA 02142

Allen Strange, **Electronic Music: Systems, Techniques, and Controls**, Wm. C. Brown Company, 135 S. Locust St., Dubuque, IA 52001

John Strawn, Editor, **Digital Audio Signal Processing: An Anthology**, William Kaufmann, Inc., 95 First St., Los Altos, CA 94022

The Synthesizer (4 volume set), Roland, 7200 Dominion Circle, Los Angeles, CA 90040

Synthesizer Basics, Hal Leonard Publishing Corp., 8112 W. Bluemound Rd., Milwaukee, WI 53213

Synthesizer Techniques, Hal Leonard Publishing Corp., Milwaukee, WI 53213

Synthesizers and Computers, Hal Leonard Publishing Corp., Milwaukee, WI 53213

Thomas Wells and Eric Vogel, **The Technique of Electronic Music**, Sterling Swift Publishing, Box 188, Manchaca, TX 78652

The Whole Synthesizer Catalog, Hal Leonard Publishing Corp., Milwaukee, WI 53213

ACKNOWLEDGEMENTS

I wish to thank the following people and companies for their part in making this book possible: Larry Fast of Synergy; Keith Sharp of Inacomp; Allen Dresser of Mega Music; Gary Osteen and Jay Sterrett of Micro Music; Ben Bradley, computer whiz; Jim Henriques, physicist; Earnie Earnest and Marcus Graham of DigiTraks; Craig Anderton of *Electronic Musician*; Russ Coffman of Desktop Publishing Consultants; Steve Grom of Fender Musical Instruments; the entire staff of *Keyboard* magazine; the International MIDI Association; Robert Moog; Lee Sebel, Nancy Kewin, and Barbi Clark of Roland; Yamaha International; Oberheim; J.L. Cooper Electronics; E-mu Systems; Ensoniq; Akai; New England Digital; Korg USA; Fairlight Instruments; Sequential; Europa Technology; and special thanks to my parents, and to Suzanne and Marisa, for their patience, faith, and encouragement.

The front cover photograph is by Doug Shiver.
The back cover photo is courtesy of RolandCorp US.

INDEX